PSYCHOLOGY OF THE PLANETS

Also published by ASTRO COMPUTING SERVICES

The American Atlas
The American Book of Tables
The American Ephemeris for the 20th Century (Midnight)
The American Ephemeris for the 20th Century (Noon)
The American Ephemeris for the 21st Century
The American Ephemeris 1901 to 1930
The American Ephemeris 1931 to 1980 & Book of Tables
The American Ephemeris 1941 to 1950
The American Ephemeris 1951 to 1960
The American Ephemeris 1961 to 1970
The American Ephemeris 1971 to 1980
The American Ephemeris 1981 to 1990
The American Ephemeris 1991 to 2000
The American Sidereal Ephemeris 1976 to 2000
The American Heliocentric Ephemeris 1901 to 2000
Basic Astrology: A Guide for Teachers and Students (Negus)
Basic Astrology: A Workbook for Students (Negus)
Interpreting the Eclipses (Jansky)
The American Book of Charts (Rodden)
Astrological Insights Into Personality (Lundsted)
The Fortunes of Astrology (Granite)
Planetary Planting (Riotte)
Planting by the Moon (Best & Kollerstrom)
The Only Way to . . . Learn Astrology, Vol. I
    Basic Principles (March & McEvers)
The Only Way to . . . Learn Astrology, Vol. II
    Math & Interpretation Techniques (March & McEvers)
The Lively Circle (Koval)

PSYCHOLOGY
OF
THE PLANETS

francoise
gauquelin

International Standard Book Number 0-917086-32-5
Printed in the United States

Cover design by Laurie Garner

Printed by McNaughton & Gunn

Published by Astro Computing Services
P.O. Box 16430
San Diego, CA 92116

Also, Distributed by Para Research, Inc.
Whistlestop Mall
Rockport, MA 01966

ACKNOWLEDGMENTS

My warmest thanks to Neil Michelsen, President of Astro Computing Services and Thomas Shanks, Director of Research, for their assistance.

TABLE OF CONTENTS

TABLES

FIGURES

THE
PSYCHOLOGY
OF
THE
PLANETS

FOREWORD

In 1973, in *Cosmic Influences on Human Behavior*, I wrote:

> Our everday language has preserved the astrological meanings of the planets. Consider, for example, these dictionary definitions (Webster):
>> **Saturnine:** supposed to be born under the influence of the planet Saturn which tends to make people morose; of a gloomy temper; heavy; grave
>>
>> **Martial:** from Mars, the God of War; military; warlike
>>
>> **Jovial:** because the planet Jupiter was believed to make those born under it of a jovial temperament: merry, joyous, jolly.
>
> Likewise the words *mercurial, moony, lunatic,* and *venereal* are part of our everyday vocabulary. Planetary symbolism is firmly anchored in our minds.

This does not automatically mean that these traditional influences are real. A quarter of a century ago, after my first book, *L'Influence des Astres (The Influence of the Stars)*, I asked myself if there exists some truth to planetary symbolism. In our research we found Mars prominent at the birth of military men and sports champions, Jupiter prominent for actors, Saturn for scientists and the Moon for poets. In reality, most military men or athletes are martial, most actors jovial, most scientists saturnine and most poets moonish. From these results I developed the feeling that there might be something significant. This feeling needed to be vindicated by objective scientific control. How, then, could we proceed? Before 1970, there was no method for testing planetary symbolism.

Fortunately, we soon developed a procedure for objectively analyzing planetary temperaments — the Character Traits Method. This method permitted us to identify the psychological patterns that correspond to the rise and culmination of the planets at birth. Consequently, Mars, Jupiter, Saturn, Moon and Venus temperaments were clearly defined and published from our trait catalog consisting of more than 50,000 trait units, matched with the planetary positions at the time of birth of the persons who display these traits. With this method, it became possible to compare astrological tradition with the thousands of traits in our catalog, and test the traits the astrologers ascribe to planets that are *strong* in the sky at birth.

Initially, I felt that this research would confirm astrological meanings attributed to at least a certain percentage of the planetary symbols. Some years ago, in *Cosmic Influences on Human Behavior*, I published a sketchy analysis that strongly suggests this conclusion. However, due to the pressures of work, month after month passed as I postponed attempting a more serious appraisal.

Finally, in 1978, my wife, Françoise, decided to undertake the project. Using the data from our trait catalogs, she tested the planetary symbolism defined by ten astrologers. To her astonishment — and she was skeptical — the outcome of her very elaborate study left no doubt: there is some validity to the interpretation of the ancient planetary symbols. Results showed a high degree of accuracy for qualities attributed to the Moon, Venus, Mars, Saturn, less so for Jupiter, and inconclusive results for the other planets. Nevertheless, the main conclusion of this study was extremely important. For more than twenty centuries, and despite many errors, astrology has conveyed some truths, although the real meaning is not yet clear to my scientifically oriented mind. Like Françoise, I must accept the facts: **a high percentage of the meanings ascribed to the planetary symbols, have an objective reality.**

Those who believe in astrology will probably consider the conclusions of this study terribly obvious. The skeptics, on the other hand, will probably think that Françoise finally succumbed to the charms of astrological traditions. Opinions do not matter. For the first time, scientific proof of the existence of the astrological reality of some of the planetary symbols has been clearly demonstrated. The fact that astrologers continue to misinterpret the horoscope is another issue. Françoise has brought to light the cold, hard statistical data that holds out to us, the scientists, a somewhat "different" universe. The planetary symbolism described twenty centuries ago by Claudius Ptolemy, is not an image, but a reality. People born under Saturn really are *saturnine,* under Mars, really *martial*, under Jupiter really *jovial.* Who can explain how ancient people possessed these strange clues to the universe? Possibly, in a later book, Françoise?

Michel Gauquelin

Chapter 1

PLANETS & PERSONALITY?

Why this study?

When I began this study, I was very skeptical. To me, occultism was an absurdity and I did not intend to waste my time proving it true.

My training in psychology began in Geneva, Switzerland, my home country. Later, the fame of the Sorbonne University lured me to Paris. There a strange fate awaited me in the person of Michel Gauquelin, also a student of psychology and statistics, and secretly dedicated to investigating astrology. After some prodding, he finally confessed where he was disappearing to each Thursday afternoon, busily compiling files of complete birth data on the worst criminals in the annals of the French Police. Furthermore, his principal weekend activity was to calculate chart after chart to test the truth of astrological writings.

I was simultaneously baffled and filled with admiration. The topic of this research seemed senseless, but his objective methods seduced me. I longed for a husband who would accept my collaboration in scientific research and had found, until then, only wooers for a "stay-at-home," domestic wife. Michel accepted my participation in the research on his subjects. Without hesitation, I embarked on this adventure, certain that there was no risk involved. With objective methods, nothing positive could turn up from such a crazy enterprise. After a brief period of astrological verification, I hoped to convince Michel to abandon his projects for more quiet academic research within a normal curriculum at the Sorbonne. Our meetings developed into animated discussions about such things as how to properly divide the diurnal movement of the planets into thirty-six sectors, in which direction the sectors had to be numbered, and so on.

But my confidence in the quick effect of objective methods was too optimistic: the adventure proved to be much longer and much more difficult than I had expected. It has never ended. In this book I will describe one of the many facets of our research, the most recent and unanticipated results that the stars held in store for me.

High Peaks After Rise & Culmination

In Michel's first tests, and in several subsequent trials, classical astrological aphorisms such as the influence of the natal Sun-sign, Moon-sign, Ascending sign, aspects, transits and houses, proved to be no more reliable than chance. I was reassured. However, an unexpected and odd variation appeared in a great number of tests: significant clusters of some planetary positions after rise and culmination and, although less so, after setting and lower culmination. Figure 1, a summation of all results obtained before 1960, clearly illustrates this phenomenon.

The clusters of planetary positions after horizon and meridian axes appeared again and again in the data for notable personalities of the same profession. For example, the most renowned sports champions were born with Mars rising or culminating[1]; the most famous actors with Jupiter in these positions[2]; the most outstanding scientists with Saturn rising or culminating.[3]

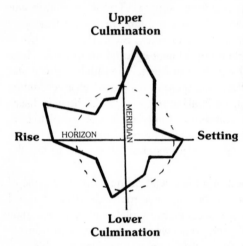

Upper Culmination

Rise

Setting

Lower Culmination

Figure 1

Clusters of planetary positions appear after the Horizon and Meridian axes at the moment of birth of outstanding professionals.

(Michel Gauquelin, *Les Hommes et les Astres*, Denoël, Parils)

When we tested ordinary people of the same professions, the results showed no cluster grouping. Thus, it was not the profession itself that showed a correspondence to the cosmic forces, but something much more individual. We concluded that the strength of character and not merely fate, gives each of the renowned personages of our samples the capability to succeed at the highest level in his occupation. Webster defines the word "personage" as "a notable or distinguished person," and "a conspicuous character," in an otherwise ordinary person. Similarly, our planetary research provides results on *distinguished notables* and *conspicuous characters*. Since a method for testing this importance of the character had not yet been devised, we had to create one.

The Trait Catalogs

Our next research concerned itself with the verification of family data.

[1]All the data of this experiment are published in *Sports Champions, Series A*, Vol. 1, (Paris: Laboratoire d'Etude des Relations entre Rhythmes Cosmiques et Psychophysiologiques, 1970).
[2]*Actors and Politicians, Series A*, Vol. 5, (Paris: Laboratoire d'Etude des Relations entre Rhythmes Cosmiques et Psychophysiologiques, 1970).
[3]*Men of Science, Series A*, Vol. 2, (Paris: Laboratoire d'Etude des Relations entre Rhythmes Cosmiques et Psychophysiologiques, 1970).

This eventually proved a genetic basis for given personality types.[4]

The next step was to investigate the actual personality factors.[5] Our method consisted of consulting biographical works describing the personalities of the notables whose birth data we already possessed. These descriptions usually provided certain character traits such as: *amiable, ambitious, self-willed.* Each stated character trait was entered on an index card together with the birth data of the notable whom it described. In this way, the birth data and personality traits were associated in an objective, verifiable context.

Thousands of cards were completed and filed in alphabetical order. These became our trait catalogs, later published in four successive volumes of our *Psychological Monographs, Series C*, Vol. 2-5. The birth data associated with the biographical traits, a collection of more than 50,000 units, became a very useful tool for research into character. An individual chart, for example, could be drawn for each of these units, and many astrological hypotheses tested against them.

The Character Traits Method

Our previous research with professional notables showed a relationship between planets and profession. In our opinion, however, the relationship was stronger between the planets and personality. To test this hypothesis, we had to study the position of the planets at the moment of birth of individuals with atypical personality. Objective criteria for separating typical from atypical personalities were developed and the character traits tested against them.

Many coaches have described the typical psychological profile of an athlete. Noting the traits contained in such descriptions, we checked to see if they appeared in our trait catalogs. (Traits are noted in these catalogs with the birth data of individuals they describe in a biography.) In the champions' group, the planet Mars was prominent. So we noted the position of Mars at the births of the individuals possessing those traits typical of athletes. We compared the collection of Mars positions, corresponding to these traits, to the Mars positions for the whole sports champion group.

The Typical Traits Lists

Figure 2 illustrates the outcomes of the three collections of Mars positions. The athletes described by traits typically considered necessary for success in sports, for instance *tenacious, courageous, tough-minded* (see curve 1 of the figure), were born with Mars rising or culminating twice as often as the general group of sportsmen (see curve 2 of the same figure). The individuals described by atypical traits such as *lazy, easygoing, tender-*

---

[4]*See Gauquelin, M. & F., Birth and Planetary Data Gathered Since 1949, Series B*, Vol. 1-6, (Paris: Laboratoire d'Etude des Relations entre Rhythmes Cosmiques et Psychophysiologiques, 1970).

[5]*See Gauquelin, M. & F. Psychological Monographs, Series C*, Vol. 2-5, (Paris: Laboratoire d'Etude des Relations entre Rhythmes Cosmiques et Psychophysiologiques, 1974-1977).

minded, etc. (see curve 3 of the figure), had no more Mars positions after rise and culmination than the general population. This demonstrates that the relationship of planets to successful professionals represents only a subordinate aspect of a much stronger relationship between the planets and the actual personality.

After having tested the positions of Mars for typical and atypical champions, we did the same with other groups that had previously yielded results. The results repeatedly confirmed our hypothesis. Not only did those traits considered most typical for success in sports show the best correspondence to the planet Mars, but the most typical traits for being a successful actor also showed the best correspondence to the planet Jupiter. Likewise, the most typical traits for becoming a great scientist showed correspondence with the planet Saturn; and the most typical traits for success as a writer, to the Moon.

The planet Venus presented a more difficult problem. Although it had given very significant results in the tests for the genetic basis of personality, Venus yielded no results from the studied professional groups.[6] Consequently, we had no clue for identifying which of the traits of the catalogs were the most typical for Venus. It was necessary to utilize more sophisticated statistical methods, pondering trait by trait which ones demonstrated the strongest correspondence to Venus. Finally we obtained a list of typical traits for Venus that was much shorter than those of the preceding planets, probably because none of the adopted references sufficiently emphasized the venusian characteristics.

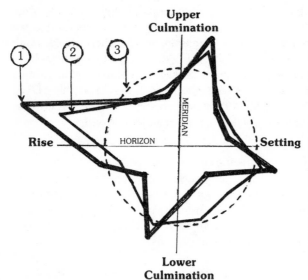

Upper Culmination

Lower Culmination

Rise

HORIZON

MERIDIAN

Setting

Figure 2
The Clusters of planetary positions after the Horizon and Meridian axes are the highest for individuals described by typical traits for their occupation (curve 1), half as high but still pronounced for the whole professional group (curve 2), and lowest for individuals described by atypical traits (curve 3).

[6]Basic documents. Gauquelin, M. & F., *Birth and Planetary Data Gathered Since 1949, Series C*, Vol. 1, (Paris: Laboratoire d'Etude des Relations entre Rhythmes Cosmiques et Psychophysiologiques, 1972).

The Sun, Mercury and the trans-Saturnian planets Uranus, Neptune and Pluto failed to produce any coherent results in our investigations. Hence, no typical traits list could be extracted for these planets.

The Most Significant Traits

It is interesting to note which traits from the data in our trait catalogs showed the most significant results. Table I lists the results for Mars, Jupiter and Saturn, in the order of their level of significance.

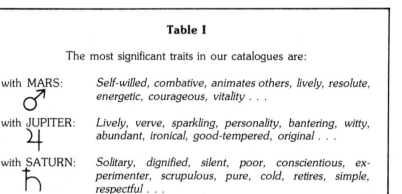

Table I

The most significant traits in our catalogues are:

with MARS: *Self-willed, combative, animates others, lively, resolute, energetic, courageous, vitality . . .*

with JUPITER: *Lively, verve, sparkling, personality, bantering, witty, abundant, ironical, good-tempered, original . . .*

with SATURN: *Solitary, dignified, silent, poor, conscientious, experimenter, scrupulous, pure, cold, retires, simple, respectful . . .*

If we compare these most significant traits with Webster's description of the **saturnine, martial** and **jovian** temperaments quoted in the Foreword of this book, we see that none of the words are identical but that, generally, they are similar. Were the first astrologers then also the first psychologists, and do their traditions convey a surprising knowledge of the psychology of personality?

Already our results seemed to confirm the old idea of a relationship between the human character and the position of the planets at birth, in favor of astrological tradition. However, great obstacles remain to trusting these traditions, the first being that none of the attributions to traditional houses were confirmed despite the fact that the houses are the very field in which we obtained results.

Chapter 2

THE PROBLEM OF HOUSES

Our division of the planetary day into 12 sectors corresponds to the traditional division of the horoscope into **houses**, with one important difference. Although the houses are traditionally numbered **counter-clockwise** like the succession of zodiacal signs, we numbered our sectors **clockwise**. This numbering follows the planetary diurnal motion, which is the astronomical factor under study.

So, as Figure 3 shows, House I corresponds to our sector 12, House II to our sector 11, House III to our sector 10 . . . and House XII to our sector 1. **Careful note should be made of this important difference between the numbering of the traditional houses and our sectors, to avoid later confusion.**

Astrologers Expect Results in Houses I and X

Traditionally, House X is said to represent *the House of public standing — the field of worldly attainment; what the world remembers a person for; position of authority, honor, and prestige; fame, profession or career.*

House I is said to be *the House of Self — the field of action and personal initiative; the personality; the character type . . . destiny in the making.*[1]

Although these definitions support our results for professional notables and their character traits, our prominent clusters of planetary positions **were not** situated in the above mentioned Houses. House X corresponds to sector 3 and House I to sector 12. Both consistently were devoid of results, as shown in Figure 1.

Results Actually Appear in Houses XII and IX

What does astrological tradition say, then, of House XII, our sector 1, and House IX, our sector 4, in which our prominent results appear? M. Douglas & M. Moore's, *Astrology, the Divine Science*[2], for instance, describes Houses XII and IX as *sacrifice* and *distant land*, respectively. Although its descriptions seemed pertinent for character and career, here they evidently fail. In addition, this is one of the more recent astrology books and, therefore, does not insist on the traditionally negative implications of these Houses.

Ptolemy is more dramatic, when he describes the effects that he ex-

[1]Moore, M. & Douglas M., *Astrology, the Divine Science*, (York Harbour, ME: Arcane Publications, 1971), p. 295-296.
[2]*Ibid.*

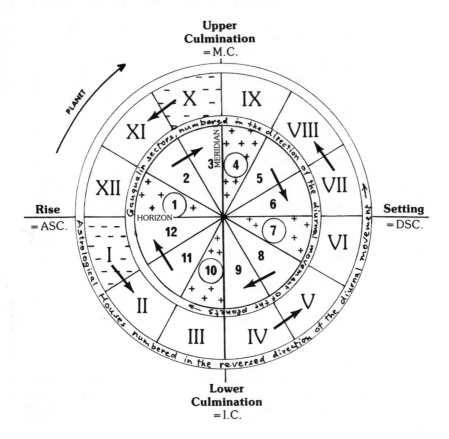

Figure 3

Prominent results do not appear in Houses I and X, but in Houses XII, IX, VI, III.
In astrological textbooks, a planetary position in House I or House X is considered
as prominent for determining character or social status of the native. But the results
with character traits did not appear in these Houses. All the significant frequencies
appear in Houses XII and IX, i.e. our sectors 1 and 4 situated after, and not before,
the axes Horizon and Meridian. Results appeared also in Houses VI and III, our
sectors 7 and 10, but they were less marked and less constant.

pects from these regions of the sky. House XII is to him a *kakos daimon* —an evil spirit — because "it injures the emanations from the stars in it, to the earth, and the thick, misty exhalation from the moisture of the earth creates such a turbidity and, as it were, an obscurity, that the stars do not appear in either their true color or magnitude."[3]

Of the planets in House IX he writes that they start falling from Midheaven to the Occident, after having reached House X, the highest point in the sky. Houses VI and III, our prominent sectors 7 and 10, are neglected by Ptolemy together with all the invisible part of the sky, considering that "the whole region below the earth must, as is reasonable, be disregarded."[4]

This attempt by Ptolemy to rationalize the traditionally unfavorable meaning attributed to the **cadent** Houses, XII, IX, VI and III, does not bar the fact that in these very houses — our sectors 1, 4, 7, 10 — the planetary positions are linked with successful professionals who display a vivid personality. This is surely not encouraging for trusting the tradition. Only the emphasis placed on the Horizon and Meridian axes is corroborated by the statistics.

Using this ancient intuition, the favorable **zones** should have been progressively expanded to thirty degrees **after** the rise and culmination of the planets, i.e., Houses XII and IX. Instead, the thirty degrees **before** the rise and culmination of the planets were adopted as more essential for knowing the native's character and social status. When will the astrological community admit that this was an error?

These and several other inadequacies reinforced my skepticism about astrological texts. Even if some keywords attributed to a planet seemed comparable to some of the traits in our typical lists, I doubted this frequency would exceed the law of chance occurrence.

The Character Trait Method provided a perfect tool for testing astrological texts. I hoped this method would reveal a total absence of relationships, thereby putting an end to abusive comparisons between our previous results and occult traditions.

Nevertheless, the Astrologers' Keywords Achieve Results

Normally, an astrological textbook devotes a chapter to describing the planets and their fields of influence. These correspondences include stones, animals, plants, meteorological events, and illnesses that tradition links to each celestial body; but obviously only the paragraphs dedicated to personality factors could be used for this study. Seventy-one astrological textbooks from Michel's abundant library provided the keywords necessary to describe the supposed planetary realms of influence. About one half of these books are written in French and the other half in English, with few ex-

---

[3]Ptolemy, C., *Tetrabiblos*, III:9-10, trans. Robbins, (Cambridge: Loeb's Classical Library, Harvard University Press, 1956).
[4]*Ibid;*

ceptions in German, Latin, Hebrew and Greek. Over the course of one winter, I thoroughly analyzed these descriptions of the planets, listing all the psychological keywords I could glean from them.

Upon completing this task, I searched our trait catalogs for the same keywords, listed with the names of the notables described in a biography by those traits, and their moment of birth. At the moment of birth of each listed notable, the planets occupy one of our thirty-six sectors. For all the keywords of an astrologer, the planetary positions in the thirty-six sectors were counted. The thirty-six frequencies thus obtained were then condensed, two-by-two, into eighteen sectors, or three-by-three into twelve sectors, latter allowing comparison with the astrological houses.

Finally, the results were tabulated! We found no relationship which tradition predicts for the transits, signs or Houses I or X. However, high peaks did appear after the rise and culmination of the five previously significant planets — Moon, Venus, Mars, Jupiter and Saturn.

Astrological tradition had not predicted the location of the results; but still, results were obtained with the astrologers own keywords. My hope to eliminate the occult traditions was destroyed. Objectively demonstrable truth exists in astrological textbooks. I could not deny it any longer.

Chapter 3

COMPUTERS TO THE RESCUE!

The first results from the astrologers' keywords were obtained by hand computation from the ten first textbooks of Michel's library, in alphabetical order. These books were not particularly good or renowned. Some descriptions of the planetary types were so short and sketchy that it seemed nothing could be expected from them. Nevertheless, they yielded results. I had to continue to check this data for statistical significance. I combined the positions of the Moon, Venus, Mars, Jupiter and Saturn to obtain confirmation that the results with the first ten tested textbooks were significant. Now I had to use much larger samples to test each body of the solar system separately.

Verification by hand is very slow and more prone to error. Human nature is fallible even when motivated by the strongest desire to avoid deficiencies. We simply needed the efficiency of machines.

To my great relief, interesting news reached us at this point from Neil Michelsen, owner of Astro Computing Services. For research purposes, ACS had stored on the computer all the birth data of the professional notables that we had published in our *Series A*, as well as all the character traits of our catalogs *Series C*. John Addey, from London, already had spent some time at Astro Computing Services researching harmonics. Neil invited us to San Diego to use his computer facilities for our research.

This generous offer eliminated the problem of slowness and human fallibility. We spent an entire year in San Diego, living in a white house two blocks away from Neil's computer. We also had the competent help of Thomas Shanks, ACS, Director of Research.

The Ten Selected Textbooks

The expanded experiments were conducted on ten books selected from Michel's library according to two criteria: their renown in the astrological community and the clarity of their keywords.

We could not, for instance, select Dane Rudhyar's *The Astrology of Personality*, despite its renown, because his descriptions of the planetary characteristics were long sentences from which no simple keywords could be derived.

Neither could most of the ancient authors be retained. Their old-fashioned terminology did not correspond to the terms of our trait catalogs.[1]

Only Ptolemy's Tetrabiblos (a French translation by Nicolas Bourdin,

[1]The ancient authors could not be used textually; but for some of them, a later investigation was based on adaptations of their terminology. See Chapter 8.

recently revised by Rène Alleau for publication in 1974) provided comparable modern psychological terms.

The following ten books were finally retained for a complete analysis of their chapter about the planets:

Tetrabiblos, Claudius Ptolemy (first publication, Second Century AD)

The Principles of Astrology, Charles E. O. Carter (first published 1925)

The Modern Textbook of Astrology, Margaret Hone (first published 1951)

Défense et Illustration de l'Astrologie, André Barbault (1955)

Astrological Keywords, Manly P. Hall (first published 1958)

Teach Yourself Astrology, Jeff Mayo (1964)

Dictionary of Astrology, Dal Lee (1968)

Keywords, Paul Grell (1970)

The Study of Astrology, Henry Weingarten (1977)

The Round Art, A.T. Mann (1978)

From the chapters about planets in these books, all the psychological terms were listed. Then I checked their presence in the trait catalogs (published in Volumes 2 through 5 of our *Series C*). As in the previous study, those keywords corresponding to catalog traits were tested using the accompanying birth data of the notables.

Two Examples of the Procedure

In Jeff Mayo's *Teach Yourself Astrology*, "The Planets: Life Principles," the Sun is the first celestial body analyzed. A brief initial description — "power of integration, wholeness of being" — conveys four possible keywords: *power, self-integration, wholeness, being*. Only one of these keywords — *power* — was listed in our catalogs, as *powerful*, an equivalent adjective. In our four catalogs we found a total of 225 notables listed under *powerful*. As a next step, we calculated the Sun's position at the moment of birth of each individual and computed the frequency of the Sun in the thirty-six sectors of the Sun's day. Would the Sun positions be significant in the **plus zones** of the 225 notables described as *powerful* by their biographers?

No. The Sun positions did not distribute throughout the key sectors in a way other than could be expected by chance. Thus, the first Sun keyword of Mayo failed to confirm the hypothesis of a relationship between the position of the Sun in a chart and the character manifested by persons described by this keyword. However, when we checked the position of the other bodies at the moment of birth of the 225 powerful people, we discovered that their combined Jupiters formed significant clusters of positions after rise and culmination. The predicted relationship between the trait *powerful* and the Sun positions was not confirmed, but an unpredicted relationship between this trait and the planet Jupiter emerged. Of course, one experiment is not sufficient proof of fact. A single result can always occur due to statistical odds and chance fluctuation. We had to continue with more checkings before drawing any conclusions.

As a second example of the way we worked, let us now examine the "Mars Life Principles" from the same chapter of Mayo's book. He describes Mars as: "Activity through enterprise, self-assertion, energetic expression." This provides also four possible keywords: *active, enterprising, assertive* and *energetic.* These four keywords are listed in our trait catalogs and correspond to the birth data of 357, 11, 62 and 258 notables, respectively. Mars revealed impressive clusters after its rise and culmination for the moments of birth of these individuals. From the start, Mars provided more promising results than the Sun.

The Body of Data

According to the procedures described above, the following numbers of keywords were extracted from the appropriate chapters of the ten selected textbooks. Unless stated otherwise, the numbers refer to the solar system bodies Mercury, Venus, Mars, Jupiter, Saturn, Uranus, Neptune, Pluto, the Sun and the Moon.

Ptolemy:	193 keywords (without keywords for Uranus, Neptune and Pluto)
Carter:	315 keywords
Hone:	251 keywords
Barbault:	442 keywords
Hall:	629 keywords (no Pluto descriptions)
Mayo:	300 keywords
Lee:	142 keywords
Grell:	498 keywords
Weingarten:	215 keywords
Mann:	260 keywords

Because small samples produce less reliable statistical results than larger ones, we see that some authors are less apt to achieve high statistical significance with their keywords than others. However, this unavoidable variation was not excessively pronounced. We did our best to include every meaningful word. Statistical treatment of this data should produce valid results.

The Statistical Treatment of the Data

Let us present here a short summary of our research methodology which is described in its entirety in our publication *Methods* and in our *Psychological Monographs*.

Observed Frequencies: Each trait from our catalog is listed with the names and birth data of the persons described by that trait in a biography. The birth positions of the ten bodies of the solar system in the thirty-six sectors of diurnal movement were listed for each individual and then added for lists of traits. The sectors that proved significant in our previous research — sectors 1, 2, 3, 9, 10, 11, 12 and 36 — are the *plus zones*, mainly situated after the rise and culmination of a planet.

Expected Frequencies: To establish the expected statistical frequencies in the thirty-six sectors, we first computed a *reference* distribution for each celestial body. Two major factors were computed: the position of the planet at the birth of each individual listed in our trait catalogs, and the number of his traits in the consulted biographies. The expected frequencies for a *tested traits list* were then calculated proportionally to the number of individuals described by the tested traits and the number of planetary positions in each sector of the reference distribution (examples of this procedure are given in Volumes 2 through 5 of our *Series C*, p. 33).

Statistical Test: The difference between observed and expected frequencies is tested by Chi Square with one degree of freedom ($\chi^2_{(1)}$) applied to:
1. The *plus zones* versus the *minus zones* (out of the thirty-six sectors, the numbers 36, 1, 2, 3, and 9, 10, 11, 12, versus other sectors)
2. Houses XII and IX versus the remaining houses, (i.e.; out of twelve sectors, the numbers 1 and 4 versus the others).

Significance Level: Tables give the probability level for each calculated Chi Square. For high Chi Square values the Tables can be used only if Chi Square was calculated on a normal group.

Our keyword lists do not generate entirely normal distributions of expected frequencies. They are often slightly biased by astronomical or demographic peculiarities and by psychological or semantic links between character traits. In these instances, the Chi Square Tables are not always adequate. Therefore, our significance levels must be interpreted only as suggesting repetition of an experiment to see if the same significance level is reached or exceeded in the same circumstances. If the initial results are not replicable, the first result must be considered a chance fluctuation without any astrological meaning.

The ten textbooks provide 290 keywords for the Sun, 279 for the Moon, 306 for Mercury, 370 for Venus, 407 for Mars, 386 for Jupiter, 409 for Saturn, 345 for Uranus (without keywords from Ptolemy), 332 for Neptune (without keywords from Ptolemy), and 121 for Pluto (without keywords from Ptolemy and Hall). The keywords are presented in the Appendix of this volume by planet and by author, to facilitate verification and control by other researchers.

Chapter 4

TESTING THE ASTROLOGERS' KEYWORDS

Ptolemy's Results

Without a doubt, the most interesting results stem from the "king of astrologers," Claudius Ptolemy, whose Tetrabiblos is still constantly quoted as the basic reference book in astrology. Parts I, II and III of the Tetrabiblos contain repeated descriptions of qualities attributed to the planets, the majority being located in *The Planets as Ruler of the Soul, Part III*, p. 14.[1]

In Figure 4 each square represents the meeting point of two factors tested for correlation. The planet keywords are on the abscissa, and the actual positions of the planets in the **plus zones**, on the ordinate.[2] In these two dimensions we can study the ten bodies of the solar system. There are one hundred squares in the graph, each with a specific result indicated by a plus sign if positive, and by a minus sign if negative. The square remains empty if the result is not significant.[3]

The first square at the top of the graph corresponds to **Sun keywords** and to **Sun positions** in the **plus zones**. The second square corresponds to **Moon keywords** and **Sun positions** in **plus zones**. The third square corresponds to **Mercury keywords** and **Sun positions** in **plus zones**, and so forth for the ten planetary keyword lists.

On the second line, the first square corresponds to the **Sun keywords** and to **Moon positions** in **plus zones.** The second square corresponds to **Moon keywords** and **Moon positions** in the **plus zones**, etc. If the astrologers' sayings are correct, we should expect a positive result in each square of the diagonal outlined in bold in Figure 4.

On the Diagonal

The first square of the diagonal is empty: the correspondence of

[1]The basic analysis of Ptolemy's keywords was done with Nicolas Bourdin's French version of the *Tetrabiblos*, because it was updated in 1974 by Rène Alleau for publication by Culture, Art, Loisir, and provided thus the greatest amount of traceable keywords in our trait catalogs. Having been criticized for this choice, I tested afterwards a parallel selection of keywords in Robbins English translation of the *Tetrabiblos*; the results were similar for Moon, Venus, Mars, Saturn; but for Jupiter they were significantly negative. This is commented on further in Chapter 10, footnote 3.

[2]As the statistical comments of p. 14 explain, we call *plus zones* the sectors containing the highest positive results in our research. They are numbered, in the division in 36 sectors of the planet's day, sectors 1, 2, 3, 9, 10, 11, 12, 36.

[3]The three last columns of the graph are empty for another reason: they correspond to Uranus, Neptune and Pluto's keywords. But these three bodies were not known at Ptolemy's time, so he gave no keywords for them. No keywords and no results, for any of the ten studied planets in these last columns.

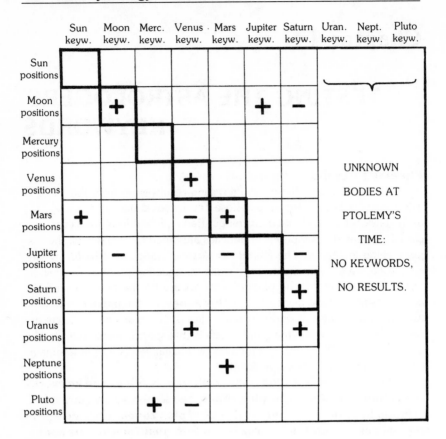

	Sun keyw.	Moon keyw.	Merc. keyw.	Venus keyw.	Mars keyw.	Jupiter keyw.	Saturn keyw.	Uran. keyw.	Nept. keyw.	Pluto keyw.
Sun positions										
Moon positions		+				+	−			
Mercury positions										
Venus positions				+						
Mars positions	+			−	+					
Jupiter positions		−			−		−			
Saturn positions								+		
Uranus positions				+			+			
Neptune positions					+					
Pluto positions			+	−						

UNKNOWN BODIES AT PTOLEMY'S TIME: NO KEYWORDS, NO RESULTS.

Figure 4

With Ptolemy's keywords, positive results appear, on the diagonal of the graph, for the Moon, Venus, Mars and Saturn, and not for the other bodies of the solar system.

How to read the figure: each square of this graph corresponds, in one direction to the keyword-list of a planet, in the other direction to the positions in *plus zones* of a planet. Thus, the first square of the top line represents the *Sun result* with *Sun keywords,* the second square represents the *Sun result* with *Moon keywords,* the third square represents the *Sun result* with *Mercury keywords,* and so forth.

The first square of the second line represents the *Moon result* with *Sun keywords,* the second square *Moon result* with *Moon keywords,* the third square *Moon result* with *Mercury keywords,* etc.

☐ →An empty square indicates that the result in *plus zones* was not significant.

⊞ →A square containing a *plus sign* indicates that the result was *positive*.

⊟ →A square containing a *minus sign* indicates that the result was *negative*.

☐ →The squares outlined on the *diagonal*, indicate that the main results are expected at the meeting point of the *same* planet's keywords and actual *plus zones* positions.

Ptolemy's keywords for the Sun, to the number of Sun positions in **plus zones**, is not significant. But the second square of the diagonal contains a plus sign: Ptolemy's keywords for the Moon correspond to a significantly positive number of Moon positions in **plus zones**. No significance was demonstrated for Mercury, but positive correlations surfaced for Venus, Mars and Saturn. Thus, four out of the five planets which gave results in our previous research also produced positive results with Ptolemy's keywords — a striking discovery!

Jupiter's results in **plus zones** are insignificant in relationship to Jupiter keywords even though they were extremely positive in our former investigations. The lack of positive results for Sun and Mercury keywords agrees with our previous results. The existence of the distant planets Uranus, Neptune and Pluto, was not known in Ptolemy's time. Therefore, we have no keywords for them and consequently, no results on the diagonal which could be compared to those of our previous investigations.[4]

Outside of the Diagonal

Our interest was also piqued by the positive and negative results that appear outside the outlined squares of the diagonal. For instance, on the second line of Figure 4, we see that the Moon shows positive correspondence not only to Ptolemy's Moon keywords (diagonal), but also to his Jupiter keywords (an important result that we must keep in mind for further discussion). On the same line, we see that the Moon generates a negative result in relation to Ptolemy's Saturn keywords — an additional outcome of interest to keep in mind.

Switching over to the line of results for Mars (fifth line), we find outside of the diagonal a positive result with Sun keywords, and a negative result with Venus keywords.

On the sixth line we have already seen that there is no positive Jupiter result with Ptolemy's Jupiter keywords (diagonal); but we find a negative result with the Moon, Mars and Saturn keywords. In the end, Jupiter does yield quite significant results.

As we explained earlier, not all significant results can be trusted after only one experiment. However, it should be noted that many of the results agree with our previous ones. We can keep them in mind for further confirmation with the other nine astrological textbooks.

The Modern Astrologers' Results

In Figure 5, we have compiled the results from all the remaining nine texts. The main results for each textbook will be found, as previously indicated, in the squares of the diagonal outlined in bold, depicting each

[4]The Uranus, Neptune and Pluto results of the graph were obtained outside of the diagonal, with the keyword lists of the other planets.

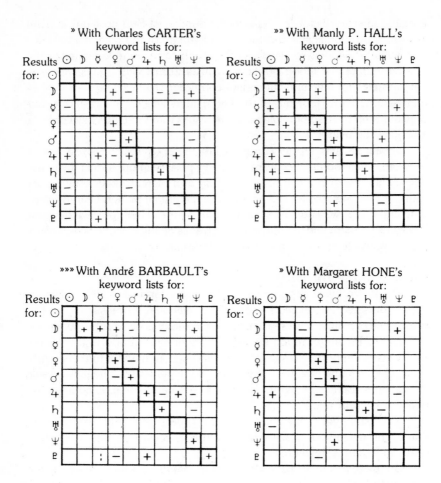

Figure 5

With the other astrologers' keywords, the results are nearly all positive for the Moon, Venus, Mars and Saturn. But nearly all the authors fail to produce positive results for the Sun, Mercury, Jupiter, and the distant planets Uranus, Neptune and Pluto. *(See page 18, Figure 4, for an explanation on interpreting these graphs.)*

»» With Dal LEE's keyword lists for:

Results for:	☉	☽	☿	♀	♂	♃	♄	♅	♆	♇
☉										
☽				−		−			+	
☿							+		+	+
♀									+	
♂			−	−	+		−			
♃		−					−	+	−	−
♄						+				
♅										
♆						−				
♇		+			−					

»»» With Henry WEINGARTEN's keyword lists for:

Results for:	☉	☽	☿	♀	♂	♃	♄	♅	♆	♇
☉								−		
☽	−	+			−	+	−		+	−
☿				−					+	
♀	−			+	−	−	−			−
♂	+	−		−		+			−	
♃	+							+	−	
♄				+				−	+	
♅		+		+						
♆										
♇							−			+

» With Jeff MAYO's keyword lists for:

Results for:	☉	☽	☿	♀	♂	♃	♄	♅	♆	♇
☉			+							
☽	−	+			−		−		+	
☿				−						
♀	−			+	−					
♂	+	−		−	+		+	−	−	
♃	+	−							−	
♄		−					+			
♅									+	
♆		+						−	+	
♇						+		+	+	

»» With Paul GRELL's keyword lists for:

Results for:	☉	☽	☿	♀	♂	♃	♄	♅	♆	♇
☉										
☽	−	+			−				+	
☿		+			−	−		+		
♀	−			+	−					
♂	+	−		−	−	+			−	
♃	−									
♄								+		
♅										
♆										
♇										

»»» With A. T. MANN's keyword lists for:

Results for:	☉	☽	☿	♀	♂	♃	♄	♅	♆	♇
☉				+		−		−		
☽	−	+			+		+			
☿	−						−			
♀	−	+		+		−				
♂	+	−		−	+		−			
♃	+	−		−	−		−			
♄						+		+	−	
♅								+		
♆				−						+
♇						+				

» Authors from U.K.
»» Authors from U.S.A.
»»» Authors aware of our results.

planets' results in **plus zones**, produced by the same planet's **keywords**.

On all nine diagonals Mars and Saturn yield positive results; Venus in eight of the diagonals, and the Moon in six. Mars and Saturn keywords reveal a 100% correlation (a striking result), Venus 90%, and the Moon keywords, 70%.

In contrast, the Sun, Mercury and Uranus squares are all empty on the diagonal. Seven of the nine diagonals reveal the same result for Neptune and Pluto. As for Jupiter, the result on the diagonal is positive only once, null six times, negative twice, and null with Ptolemy's keywords — a rather disappointing outcome for such an important body.

We concluded that for the Moon, Venus, Mars and Saturn, the lists of the modern astrologers, as that of Ptolemy, agree among themselves as well as with our former statistical results. Similarly, but in a negative way, the astrologers' keyword lists agree by an absence of results for the Sun, Mercury, and the distant planets Uranus, Neptune and Pluto. The case of Jupiter is more complex and presents quite contradictory results which we will discuss later.

This first conclusion gives us clear working hypotheses. For four out of five bodies which gave significant results in our research, the astrologers' keywords also give significant results; for the fifth body, Jupiter, their results are disconcerting; for the other bodies, the astrologers' keywords are not more successful than our statistical methods in eliciting results.

Clusters of Consistent Results

Like Figure 4, Figure 5 unveils many significant results outside the diagonals. At only a glance one cannot easily distinguish those results that are consistent among the astrologers and those that vary.

To develop a clearer picture of the consistent clusters of results throughout the ten tested textbooks, we counted, for each square in the ten graphs, the number of significant results **in the same direction** (plus or minus). This computation revealed a clearly visible fact: outside the diagonal of Figure 5, as on it, all the meaningful results in the same direction for several astrologers are situated on the lines corresponding to the Moon, Venus, Mars, Saturn and, interestingly enough, Jupiter. These five bodies of the solar system which showed results in our previous inquiries sharply contrast with the other bodies — the Sun, Mercury, Uranus, Neptune and Pluto. For these latter five not only the diagonal, but the entire line of positions in **plus zones** remains nearly empty. When a result does appear, it is usually an isolated example or coupled with a result in the opposite direction, confirming the randomness of both. Such results are probably erratic cases and we will not take them into account. Instead, we will center our discussion on the meaningful clusters of five or more results in the same direction. Such clusters appear exclusively in relationship to the Moon, Venus, Mars, Jupiter and Saturn.

Chapter 5

THE PSYCHOLOGY OF
THE PLANETS

Moon Clusters of Results

By counting how many of the ten tested authors produced a significant result, we obtained the following Table for the Moon. It shows clusters of five or more results in the same direction in relationship to planetary keywords. Some clusters are made up of positive results and others of negative results. We find no contradictory clusters containing both positive and negative results for the Moon. This indicates a good agreement among the ten author's keyword lists.

Keyword list for	SUN	MOON	MERC.	VENUS	MARS	JUP.	SAT.	URAN.	NEPT.	PLUTO
MOON result in "plus zones"	5 times negative	7 times positive			8 times negative		8 times negative		8 times positive	

The positive Moon result obtained seven times with Moon keywords has already been discussed above in the context of the graph diagonal.

A second positive cluster of results from eight of the ten tested texts appears between alleged Neptune keywords and the Moon. How is this possible since the Neptune keywords did not produce positive results for Neptune?[1] We interpret from this data that the characteristics attributed to Neptune by the astrologers are in reality lunar attributes. If we compare the keyword lists for these two bodies, we find an obvious overlap: *dreamer, sensitive, imaginative, intuitive* appear both as Moon and as Neptune keywords. Furthermore, other components of the classical Neptune personality such as *spiritualism, mystical sense, visionary, subtle*, belong to the Moon, as reflected in our statistical results (see *Typical Traits of THE MOON TEMPERAMENT*, (Paris: Laboratoire d'Etude des Relations entre Rhythmes Cosmiques et Psychophysiologiques, 1977). In reality, characteristics attributed by the astrologers to Neptune are lunar attributes. These results will be tested once again with new statistical data gathered in 1980 from U.S. documents. Meanwhile, our impression is that Moon keywords and Neptune keywords are interchangeable and contribute equally to Moon results.

We have stated above that Sun keywords do not bear out Sun results with any of the astrologers' lists. However, in relation to the Moon, the Sun keywords appear more interesting: they produce negative Moon results in

---

[1]With Neptune keywords, there are two Neptune results, one with Mayo and one with Barbault. However two results out of ten trials are not enough to eliminate the presumption of statistical odds due to astronomical biases.

five instances. This did not surprise us. The Sun keywords form a psychologically coherent picture of a personality that is clearly atypical of the Moon. On this point the astrologers will agree.

We can draw similar conclusions from the Mars and Saturn keywords: each produce negative Moon results in eight instances. This was expected since, in the beginning of our research, we observed that, in the groups in which Mars was significantly positive (sports champions, military men, physicians), the Moon was low. Inversely, in the groups in which the Moon was strong (poets, writers), Mars and Saturn were low.[2] The present negative Moon result with keywords that are typical for Mars and Saturn, thus becomes meaningful.

Venus Clusters of Results

By counting the results obtained from the ten tested authors, we find, for Venus, fewer clusters of five or more results in the same direction than for the Moon; precisely three instead of five. Nevertheless, those three clusters are instructive.

Keyword list for	SUN	MOON	MERC.	VENUS	MARS	JUP.	SAT.	URAN.	NEPT.	PLUTO
VENUS result in "plus zones"	5 times negative			9 times positive	5 times negative					

Apart from the expected Venus result with Venus keywords (nine times out of ten in the graph diagonals), tradition predicts another cluster: the negative Venus results that appear five times with Mars keywords. We could not foresee this confirmation of tradition by merely checking the keyword lists of Venus and Mars because they are not clearly antagonistic (see Appendix, pp. 71-77). However, after an inquiry based on Eysenck's personality factors, *tough-mindedness* and *tender-mindedness* we expected these results. Eysenck's personality factors produced similar antagonistic results with Mars and Venus (report to be published).

The *Sun keywords* produce also five times negative Venus results. If we examine the lists of Sun keywords from different textbooks (see the Appendix), we discover in these lists several typically Martian traits, like: *"Virile, asserts himself, aggressive, enthusiastic, powerful, restless, self-willed, energetic, full of strength . . ."* (See lists of Hone, Barbault, Mayo, Grell, Weingarten.) These traits did produce Mars results in our previous researches. We thus easily understand that they may appear here as typical anti-Venus traits, despite their attribution to the Sun by the named astrologers.

Mars Clusters of Results

Among the ten tested textbooks, we find five clusters of Mars results

[2]See Gauquelin, M., *Les Hommes et les Astres*, (Paris: Denoël, 1960), p. 143; and Vol. 1 of *Series C*, pp. 80-111.

which appeared five times or more in the same direction. These clusters will also contribute to our understanding of the Mars attributes.

Apart from the positive Mars results with *Mars keywords* that was expected on the diagonal, and appeared effectively ten times out of ten, we find other clusters which corroborate the preceding statements.

Mars gives negative results ten times out of ten with *Venus keywords,* in perfect symmetry with the negative Venus results for Mars keywords. It gives negative results five times with *Moon keywords,* another expected symmetry with the above stated negative Moon results with Mars keywords. This antagonism between Mars and the Moon appears also through the five-times negative Mars results with *Neptune keywords*; these same Neptune keywords which had given strongly positive results for the Moon (see above). And finally, we find positive Mars results on five tests with *Sun keywords,* again in symmetry with the negative Venus results produced by these same Sun keywords.

Keyword list for	SUN	MOON	MERC.	VENUS	MARS	JUP.	SAT.	URAN.	NEPT.	PLUTO
MARS result in "plus zones"	5 times positive	5 times negative		10 times negative	10 times positive				5 times negative	

All these outcomes for Mars belong to a complex, but perfectly coherent, picture that emerges from the apparently well-organized ballet of planetary couples.

Jupiter Clusters of Results

We have discovered that, contrary to other previously significant planets, the keyword lists of Jupiter did not produce coherent Jupiter results on the diagonal of the ten studied graphs. One result was positive, two negative, and seven null. Nonetheless, coherent clusters of results appeared for Jupiter in relation to keyword lists of other planets. These will contribute to our understanding of the real characteristics of Jupiter. (See Table X and XI on pp. 62 and 64.)

Keyword list for	SUN	MOON	MERC.	VENUS	MARS	JUP.	SAT.	URAN.	NEPT.	PLUTO
JUPITER result in "plus zones"	6 times positive	6 times negative							6 times negative	

Jupiter gives negative results six times with both Moon and Neptune keywords. Once again we find the Moon and Neptune coordinated in relation to a similar result. Above, their joint results were positive for the Moon; here, they are negative for Jupiter. Thus, Jupiter and the Moon demonstrate some opposed characteristics. This was not as evident in our statistical analysis of the professional groups, but seems clearly indicated here and is consequently quite enlightening.

The Jupiter data also produced positive results six times with Sun keywords. As many Sun keywords correspond to Jupiterian characteristics as to Martian ones (see results of Mars with Sun keywords). These results will appear in our later discussion of Jupiter.

Saturn Clusters of Results

Saturn presents an exceptionally pure case: on the diagonal, ten times out of ten, it correlates positively with Saturn keywords from the ten tested textbooks (as stated above). However, outside the diagonal, no other cluster of results appears in relation to the other keyword lists. The traditional qualities attributed to Saturn seem to describe Saturn quite accurately, and do not affect other planets. Consequently, no table of results is needed here.

More Tests Needed

Many interesting results surfaced in the ten graphs that represent the ten astrological textbooks, results confirmed by several repetitions so that we can accept them as valid. Others exceed the chosen level of significance either by chance or by bias unrelated to the tested hypothesis, and must be rejected. Subtle factors constantly appear and make conclusions from one statistical outcome more or less hazardous. André Barbault's *Défense et Illustration de l'Astrologie*, published in 1955, produced the best results of the ten tested textbooks, with even Jupiter significantly positive on the diagonal. Can he claim to be a better astrologer than his colleagues? According to our statistical procedures, we say, "no," because his next book, *Traité Practique d'Astrologie*, 1961, revealed a null Jupiter result. One single case never establishes a rule.

Chapter 6

AROUND THE PLANETARY DAY

Our next step was to expand our investigation from the **plus zones** (about two hours after rise and culmination) to the entire planetary day. In astrological terms, this means that, instead of studying the results of Houses XII and IX combined, we examined the pattern of all twelve houses. Astrologers, we felt, would be eager to see what results appeared directly preceding the studied Houses XII and IX, i.e., how many planetary positions showed up in Houses I and X, the houses emphasized by tradition, against our **plus zones**. All the notables' planetary positions at the moment of birth are listed in our trait catalogs and published in our *Series A*.[1] For each of these birth moments, we noted the planetary positions in corresponding divisions of the diurnal movement through the thirty-six sectors. Again, we numbered these sectors from one forward beginning with the planet's rise and proceeding clockwise in the direction of the diurnal movement (direction opposed to the traditional numbering of houses). The planetary positions were then computed for the groups of births corresponding to the keyword lists for each planet.

For instance, Ptolemy's first keyword for the Sun is *just*. In our catalogs, this trait corresponds to two champions. We noted that one of these was born with the Sun in sector eight and the other, with the Sun in sector thirty-two. Ptolemy's next keyword for the Sun, *religious*, corresponds to seventeen actors, thirty-five writers and fourteen scientists. We applied the same procedure, noting the position of the Sun in the sectors for these births; and so on for each of Ptolemy's keywords.

After calculating these Sun positions for Ptolemy's keywords, we counted the number of times the Sun occupied each sector. This computation provided frequencies for the Sun in the thirty-six sectors of the planetary day in relationship to Ptolemy's Sun keywords. Next, with these same keywords, we determined the frequencies of other planets in the thirty-six sectors.

This process was repeated with Moon keywords, then with the remaining keyword lists, until all the planetary positions in the thirty-six sectors

[1]See Gauquelin, M. & F., *Birth and Planetary Data Gathered Since 1949: Series A, Professional Notabilities*, Vol. 1-6, (Paris: Laboratoire d'Etude des Relations entre Rhythmes Cosmiques et Psychophysiologiques, 1970-1971).

had been recorded. Fortunately, Thomas Shanks and the Astro Computing Services computer assisted us in this arduous task.

Keyword Results Synthesized from the Ten Astrologers

Ten planets times ten keyword lists, times ten studied textbooks equals one thousand separate distributions of planetary positions in thirty-six sectors — quite an impressive amount of data. Even the most attentive reader would lose his wits without some organization of the data. Some grouping was necessary. We chose to combine the ten textbook frequencies by planet. Tables II and III show this synthesized compilation of the planets throughout the thirty-six sectors for the ten astrologers' combined scores. Results are only given for the planet corresponding to the keyword predictions. The 'off-diagonal' results are not represented here. Table II provides this synthesis for the five bodies which were significant in our previous research, the Moon, Venus, Mars, Jupiter and Saturn. Table III presents a synthesis of the other five bodies, the Sun, Mercury, Uranus, Neptune and Pluto. Under the name of each planet are two columns, one listing the observed frequencies, and the other the expected frequencies — a value that takes into account the astronomical and demographic distributions within the group.

Each observed frequency must be compared to the expected frequency in the same sector (see our book, *Methods*, 1957). If the observed frequency is more than the expected frequency, the result is positive; if the observed frequency is less than the expected frequency, the result is negative. To save the reader the fastidious task of calculating the difference between the observed and expected frequencies, we have presented them graphically in Figures 6 and 7. They are condensed into twelve instead of thirty-six sectors to facilitate comparisons with the twelve houses. Figure 6 shows the diagrams of the five bodies which proved significant in our previous research, and Figure 7, those of the five remaining bodies.

The Five Previously Significant Bodies

Figure 6 displays, in a line graph format, the typical effect of the five previously significant bodies after rise and culmination. Venus, Mars and Saturn produce especially high peaks after their rise; the Moon, Mars and Saturn, after their culmination. Mars additionally displays high peaks after setting and lower culmination. These high points correspond to Houses XII, IX, VI, III, as discovered in our previous investigations. Between these high points, we find low frequencies in particular for Houses I and X, despite their importance in astrology. This pattern is most pronounced with Mars.

The fifth previously significant body, Jupiter confirms its previous failure to provide predictive material. Throughout the planetary day, Jupiter's highs and lows are not very marked, contrary to the results of the four other bodies. Slightly positive after the rise and slightly negative after the culmination, Jupiter is, finally, weakly negative in **plus zones** and not significant in any sector throughout the planetary day.

TABLE II

Synthesis of the ten astrologers' results
for the bodies that we had previously found significant
and their predicted keywords.

HOUSE	SECTOR	$\mathbb{D}$ MOON obs.	exp.	♀ VENUS obs.	exp.	♂ MARS obs.	exp.	♃ JUPITER obs.	exp.	♄ SATURN obs.	exp.
XII	1	484	555.3	845	693.8	1299	636.2	677	716.1	360	353.6
XII	2	583	618.1	1161	964.8	1335	859.5	393	484.3	725	564.1
XII	3	832	571.3	1045	669.7	1737	1467.7	728	697.2	1099	678.3
XI	4	311	371.3	670	749.7	808	948.5	492	373.2	412	408.9
XI	5	378	313.1	481	483.5	954	1170.3	650	628.1	462	612.5
XI	6	167	242.3	296	420.6	428	692.9	524	561.9	492	543.6
X	7	703	836.4	593	815.5	1068	1564.8	653	670.9	502	503.3
X	8	440	422.1	503	483.1	927	1016.8	784	647.1	801	857.5
X	9	317	341.6	541	453.5	393	598.3	513	467.3	1096	910.3
IX	10	451	318.3	772	753.2	1393	967.3	634	568.0	838	585.5
IX	11	583	485.4	462	477.9	1004	874.7	717	736.4	440	377.7
IX	12	581	547.1	416	334.2	1311	986.0	605	599.6	605	486.6
VIII	13	421	470.2	525	527.8	637	779.2	563	599.7	615	742.2
VIII	14	173	268.6	167	212.8	693	952.8	465	525.6	579	625.4
VIII	15	449	443.7	448	514.3	395	600.0	449	519.4	465	521.7
VII	16	313	267.5	167	230.2	945	954.1	546	562.6	397	356.7
VII	17	381	368.2	560	510.0	1187	1247.3	406	430.5	305	311.2
VII	18	462	369.5	472	418.8	1029	1145.1	529	479.4	435	521.1
VI	19	250	374.5	290	310.6	996	1022.4	573	591.6	793	669.5
VI	20	453	404.9	464	431.1	812	532.3	576	594.4	437	512.0
VI	21	536	501.9	405	456.9	1199	823.9	477	453.0	453	608.4
V	22	385	340.1	546	477.6	662	464.7	381	402.2	298	353.6
V	23	413	471.1	390	331.0	786	1054.3	467	446.3	273	427.1
V	24	436	519.5	559	588.2	746	1105.3	412	380.0	446	458.4
IV	25	482	384.3	362	289.5	605	599.5	716	765.1	362	464.0
IV	26	433	494.5	482	554.7	612	607.0	426	510.2	416	463.7
IV	27	373	347.3	506	657.2	476	614.6	571	494.1	391	344.8
III	28	504	601.3	363	532.3	2110	1379.3	743	682.3	359	288.6
III	29	297	267.9	276	428.1	1011	867.6	564	576.2	598	721.0
III	30	578	660.9	634	674.3	1104	903.8	590	648.4	548	649.7
II	31	546	536.9	467	607.3	584	1086.3	478	498.5	263	249.1
II	32	323	306.1	402	335.9	469	683.5	422	455.1	834	676.2
II	33	681	592.6	566	378.2	865	1140.2	659	499.8	557	664.9
I	34	367	479.4	558	609.8	784	815.1	409	483.6	608	785.0
I	35	432	440.5	657	726.8	804	933.5	726	708.7	210	280.2
I	36	245	229.1	432	380.1	643	715.9	639	699.9	712	564.1
N		15763		18483		32811		20157		19186	

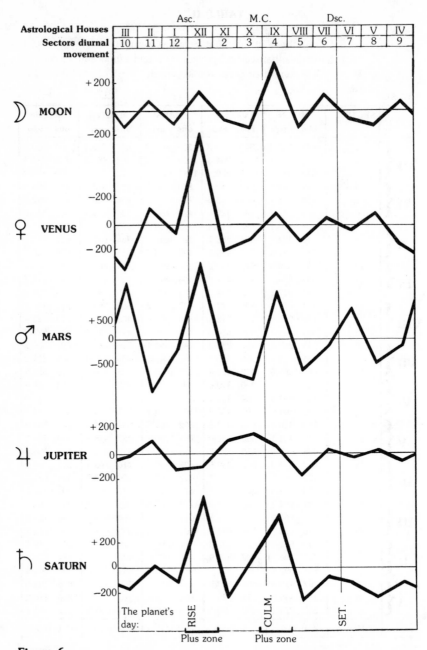

Figure 6

The five previously significant bodies all around the clock. The thin straight 0 line represents the expected frequencies for each body; the thick line going up and down along this line represents the observed frequencies in the twelve sectors (or Houses) of the planet's day.

The Five Bodies Previously Not Significant

Five celestial bodies were not significant in our previous research: the Sun, Mercury, Uranus, Neptune and Pluto. Is it that our tests were not sufficiently powerful or not properly designed to test their effect? Would the astrologers' keywords prove more successful?

One could argue that these bodies might be statistically different from the five significant bodies for physical reasons. First, the Sun is not a planet, but a star; second, Mercury is the smallest planet of our solar system, third, Uranus, Neptune and Pluto are the most distant bodies. The probability that these might show an effect of the same magnitude as the more proximate bodies does not seem equitable. We know already that their results in **plus zones** were disappointing. Table III and Figure 7 give the frequencies for the Sun, Mercury, Uranus, Neptune and Pluto throughout the thirty-six sectors and the twelve houses, respectively.

The Sun is Not Significant

For the Sun, the lack of result in plus zones is evident. Negative after the rise and slightly positive after culmination, the addition of both of the Sun's **plus zones** yields distinctly negative results in relation to the astrologers' Sun keywords, and even more so with the traditionally privileged Houses I and X. Near the lower culmination (Houses III and IV) strong deviations from the expected frequencies follow the demographic rhythm of births, a well known terrestrial fact without astrological implications. The same demographic correction has been applied to the Sun's distribution as to those of other planets; however, this procedure is not potent enough to entirely account for the extremely strong solar deviations from the mean because we do not have, with the Sun, a normal (Gaussian) distribution.

It seems reasonable to abandon the idea that the astrologers' keywords can provide results for the Sun not uncovered in our previous research.

The Smallest & Most Distant Planets Remain a Puzzle

Mercury, Uranus, Neptune and Pluto do not reveal an exceptional or distinctive pattern (Figure 7). However, we can identify a slight tendency to show positive frequencies after most of their rises and culminations. Knowing that these bodies are small or distant, we did not expect strong effects. Rather than neglect their weak tendencies because they are far from significant, we raised the question, "Is this the beginning of an effect that will appear again in other experiments and become significant with more data?"

To better assess their collective contribution, we added their frequencies in the twelve sectors and found a peak to appear after their common culmination. After their rise, however, the frequency remained very close to the mean. If added, the sectors after rise and culmination (Sector 1 plus Sector 4, or House XII plus House IX) barely reach the 0.01 level of significance. This result was obtained by an *a posteriori* addition and therefore cannot be considered scientific proof. What is more, the highest frequencies of the distribution are not situated in **plus zones**, as Figure 8

TABLE III

Synthesis of the ten astrologers' results
for the bodies that we had previously found significant
and their predicted keywords.

HOUSE	SECTOR	☉ SUN		☿ MERCURY		♅ URANUS		♆ NEPTUNE		♇ PLUTO	
		obs.	exp.	obs.	exp.	obs.	exp.	obs.	exp.	obs.	exp.
XII	1	629	584.7	299	239.5	438	317.6	236	345.3	98	107.7
	2	928	921.7	782	781.5	502	425.7	354	361.6	61	60.9
	3	632	817.4	457	462.4	452	498.0	543	473.6	135	119.7
XI	4	522	590.5	346	362.4	931	806.1	985	754.5	121	145.9
	5	955	947.9	566	608.9	453	350.2	1142	933.6	65	94.0
	6	417	432.5	408	364.6	179	249.1	452	444.2	158	124.5
X	7	931	987.4	477	553.8	407	313.1	387	381.2	100	96.1
	8	532	657.1	424	429.4	681	748.5	431	386.9	84	69.9
	9	560	426.7	237	239.5	263	414.3	564	640.1	78	82.4
IX	10	472	505.7	297	231.2	423	460.2	756	597.1	175	161.7
	11	524	673.1	488	543.6	631	540.1	352	379.7	202	143.9
	12	751	545.5	475	438.1	699	761.1	659	619.3	117	97.3
VIII	13	537	458.1	275	325.5	498	502.9	580	701.8	157	132.5
	14	495	508.1	301	244.9	386	459.0	315	339.1	68	104.6
	15	404	468.6	186	216.7	556	655.5	731	6761.4	90	89.4
VII	16	421	419.7	474	482.8	412	384.6	564	561.3	145	139.9
	17	302	281.7	264	251.4	737	501.2	322	396.1	58	84.9
	18	502	447.7	586	470.5	306	370.0	418	529.2	117	122.9
VI	19	577	734.4	157	231.4	327	318.4	318	391.4	85	109.1
	20	144	154.3	119	145.0	423	383.9	502	542.9	68	61.8
	21	387	469.4	405	370.2	240	351.8	492	490.3	111	91.0
V	22	412	382.1	353	311.0	694	651.8	690	566.3	130	111.9
	23	482	652.0	301	331.5	900	811.9	603	465.6	100	82.7
	24	494	580.5	400	441.8	653	645.5	762	751.9	119	139.0
IV	25	1747	1184.7	394	309.5	486	450.4	466	487.7	189	179.5
	26	247	279.3	407	326.0	467	471.5	423	580.5	73	117.8
	27	172	228.6	402	416.3	427	497.5	866	738.2	78	91.6
III	28	124	158.1	345	394.2	647	627.6	527	468.1	63	58.1
	29	838	732.6	269	254.4	581	460.9	430	322.1	96	79.8
	30	998	840.3	260	314.8	769	796.2	425	512.0	62	70.7
II	31	836	931.3	610	573.2	373	392.4	336	444.9	142	141.2
	32	986	764.1	582	645.3	370	403.6	415	608.0	81	103.0
	33	1070	1055.0	528	470.2	341	459.4	292	343.2	153	116.8
I	34	521	638.3	592	718.7	394	450.4	432	482.6	103	105.9
	35	616	680.6	426	376.4	396	512.2	734	704.4	49	80.3
	36	629	654.9	464	480.4	524	422.9	475	472.9	30	42.9
	N	21794		14356		17966		18979		3761	

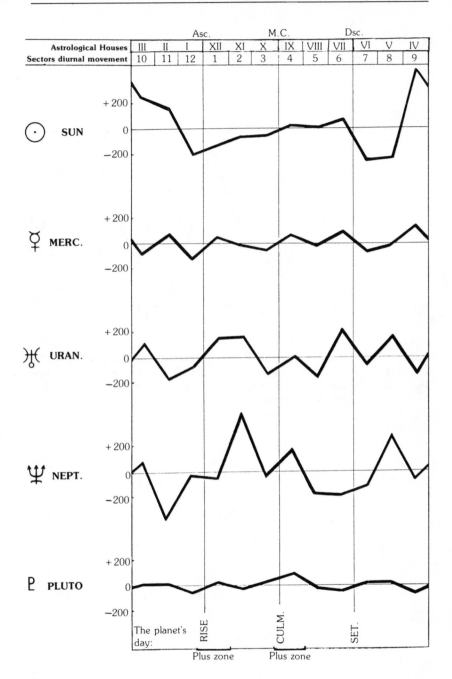

Figure 7
The five previously significant bodies all around the clock. The thin straight 0 line
represents the expected frequencies for each body; the thick line going up and down
along this line represents the observed frequencies in the twelve sectors (or Houses)
of the planet's day.

demonstrates. The highest peaks are in the irrelevant Sectors 2 and 8, instead of Sectors 1 and 4 of the twelve-sector distribution.

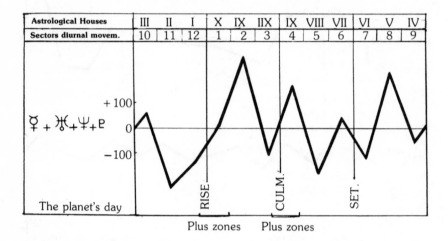

Figure 8
Are the planets Mercury, Uranus, Neptune and Pluto significant in "plus zones" if we add them? Their frequency after rise and culmination is positive, but the highest peaks of the distribution are not in sectors 1 and 4, but in the irrelevant sectors 2 and 8 of the twelve-sector distribution.

Chapter 7

HOW RIGHT ARE
THE ASTROLOGERS?

In our first studies we tested the astrologers' keywords against the positions of the planets at the moments of birth of the personalities described by these keywords. However, this is not the only method available for testing the accuracy of astrological keywords. Nor should it be considered the best method in that it presents the disadvantage of some keywords being tested with hundreds of data, and others with only one or two. For instance, the keyword *active* was used 357 times to describe notable professionals from our collection. Consequently, we were able to check hundreds of birth data. Other keywords such as *likes his home* or *lugubrious* or *skunk* appeared only once in the studied biographies. Psychologically, the seldom-used traits are no less valuable than those used frequently. In our second experiment with the astrologers' keywords we gave the same weight to each keyword by tabulating each only once.

This was done in the following way. Each keyword that was present in our traits catalogs was compared to our lists of Typical and Opposed Traits for the four significant planets Mars, Jupiter, Saturn and the Moon (see our *Psychological Monographs*). If the keyword of a planet appeared among the typical traits linked with the same planet, we noted this as a **coherency** between the astrologer's opinion and our statistical results. If the keyword of a planet appeared among the traits opposed to the same planet or among the typical traits of another planet, we noted this as an **incoherency** between the astrologer's opinion and our statistical results. (This being only a brief summary of a more complex procedure, please refer to *Correlation* 1,1 and 2,1 for more details).

Table IV demonstrates this procedure, utilizing Dal Lee's short descriptions of Jupiter as an example.

Only four planets could be tested for **coherencies** and **incoherencies** with our Typical Traits Lists: the Moon, Mars, Jupiter and Saturn. Our list of typical and opposed traits is presently too short and too tentative to allow such a test for Venus (Gauquelin, 1978). For the remaining bodies of the solar system, Uranus, Neptune and Pluto, we have never obtained significant results that would provide us with lists of typical traits.

Table V summarizes the proportions of **coherencies** obtained for the Moon, Mars, Jupiter and Saturn.

Coherencies from the Ten Selected Textbooks
At the end of each line, Table V gives the percentage of coherencies

TABLE IV

From Dal Lee's *Dictionary of Astrology* we extracted eighteen **Jupiter** keywords that appear in our trait catalogs:

Page 154: *personality, jovial, happy, expansive*

Page 158: *beneficent, expansive, noble, sincere, kind, religious, honorable, faithful, extravagant, conceited, gambler, hypocritical, fanatical*

Page 159: expansive

Nine of these keywords are present in the List of Typical Traits in our publication *The Jupiter Temperament* (Gauquelin, 1974b, pp. 73-79): *personality, jovial, happy, expansive, extravagant, conceited, gambler, expansive.*

We labeled these **plus** keywords and put them into the group of **coherencies.**

Four keywords — *noble, sincere, honorable, faithful* — present in the list of Opposed Traits in the same *Jupiter Temperament* (Gauquelin, 1974, pp. 88-93), were labeled **minus** keywords and classified **incoherencies**.

We classified two other keywords — *kind* and *religious* — from our *List of Typical Traits for the Moon* (Gauquelin 1977, pp. 66-71) as **incoherencies** and labeled them **Mo**. Lastly, we gave the label **Ma** to the keyword *fanatical*, from our *List of Typical Traits for Mars* (1973, pp. 80-81).

The **coherencies** totaled nine and the **incoherencies**, seven, for Dal Lee's Jupiter description. These results — **50% coherencies** versus **46% incoherencies** — equal nearly 50% for each kind. These proportions would indicate that Dal Lee's *Dictionary of Astrology* **does not** present a clear picture of the Jupiterian qualities that appear to be significant in our studies.

For **Saturn**, Dal Lee's *Dictionary of Astrology* gives the following keywords that also appear in our trait catalogs:

Page 154: *sadness*

Page 158: *experienced, limited, wise, reflective, careful, fearful, economical, laborious, chaste, morose, suspicious, nervous, jealous, timid, fatalistic*

Page 159: *restrained*

We found nine of these seventeen keywords — *sadness, wise, reflective, careful, fearful, economical, laborious, morose, timid* — in our traits list in *The Saturn Temperament* (Gauquelin, 1974 a, pp. 72-75). These we labeled **coherencies**.

None of these keywords appear in the List of Opposed Traits for Saturn nor in the Typical Lists of other planets. Thus, there are **no incoherencies**.

Nine coherencies versus **no incoherencies** renders proportions of **100% coherencies** versus **30% incoherencies**. Dal Lee's *Dictionary of Astrology* presents a very clear picture of the Saturn qualities that appear significant in our statistics.

obtained from each textbook. For instance, Ptolemy's *Tetrabiblos* produced a total of 53% coherencies for the Moon, Mars, Jupiter and Saturn. Therefore, Ptolemy's keywords contain 47% incoherencies. Carter's keywords reveal 55% coherencies versus 45% incoherencies, etc. In calculating these percentages, only the words scored as coherent or incoherent are considered. The keywords which do not appear on any of our lists are not counted.

In this test, Weingarten's *The Study of Astrology* (1977) yields the highest scores with 85% coherencies versus only 15% incoherencies. Should we conclude that this astrologer is more intuitive than his colleagues or that, when he wrote this book, he simply took into account the trait lists published by our laboratory? Both conclusions favor this author's adaptability.

From the bottom line of Table V one can see that Saturn has the highest score and Jupiter the lowest, as in the previous test. However, this time the percentage of coherencies for Jupiter exceeds the mean (50%) with 58% coherencies, versus 42% incoherencies. In the previous test, Jupiter scored under the mean. The keyword lists for Jupiter contain a fair amount of correct traits that need further analysis and identification, a process to be demonstrated shortly.

However, let us first continue to use the proportions of coherencies to check yet another interesting problem: has astrological knowledge regressed or progressed through time?

TABLE V

Ten astrologers' keywords for the Moon, Mars, Jupiter and Saturn:
Comparison with our *typical lists*

N = Number of astrologers' keywords that are present in our traits catalog
+ = Number of keywords that are in our *typical lists*
– = Number of keywords that are in the *opposed lists*
Mo, Ma, Ju, Sa = Number of keywords that belong to the *typical list* of another planet than the tested one.

Tested astrologer (chronological order)	MOON						MARS						JUPITER						SATURN						Percentage of coherencies
	N	+	–	Ma	Ju	Sa	N	+	–	Ma	Ju	Sa	N	+	–	Ma	Ju	Sa	N	+	–	Ma	Ju	Sa	
Ptolemy (2nd Century AD)	16	6	0	0	1	0	29	9.5	0	1	12	0	38	12	4	9	0	3	33	15.5	4	1	1	2	53%
Carter (1925)	36	14	6	0	1	6	41	17	1	0	16	0	46	18	4	4	3	1	25	10	3	0	2	2	55%
Hone (1951)	14	7	3	0	1	0	41	22	0	0	7	0	21	15	0	2	0	0	27	11	3	0	2	0	75%
Barbault (1955)	44	27	1	0	1	0	39	17	0	0	9	0	42	20	1	2	1	2	67	21.5	2	3	2	2.5	76%
Hall (1958)	73	29	6	1	4	3	88	34	3	1	14	3	80	24	17	5	0	2	71	35	5	0	2	2	65%
Mayo (1964)	20	9	1	0	0	1	40	21	1	0	6	0	23	10	2.5	2	0	3	42	16	5	1	3	2	67%
Lee (1968)	12	6	2	0	2	1	16	9	0	0	4	0	18	9	4	1	2	0	17	9	0	0	0	0	67%
Grell (1970)	31	14	4	0	2	1	61	28	0	0	10	0	71	25	10	11	4	0	60	36	5	3	0	0	67%
Weingarten (1977)	17	12	3	0	0	0	40	20	0	0	5	0	20	13	0	2	0	0	31	19	1	0	0	0	85%
Mann (1979)	22	8	2	0	0	0	25	5	0	2	6	1	30	9	3	2	2	0	35	13	2	2	1	1	59%
Percentage of coherencies	71%						64%						58%						74%						

Chapter 8

COMPARING ANCIENT & MODERN AUTHORITIES

Those who believe in the revelation of the astrological knowledge in ancient times, by higher intelligences from elsewhere, contend that astrology slowly degenerated through the centuries. But the percentage of coherencies given in Table V in chronological order of text publication, show an improvement rather than a deterioration through time: the five first percentages are slightly lower than the five last ones. This suggests a slowly developing tradition based on innumerable observations as opposed to an ancient revelation of already perfect knowledge. We tried to test both hypotheses by analyzing a greater number of ancient textbooks, despite two major difficulties with vocabulary and the way of explaining concepts that evolved through the centuries. We therefore had to translate some expressions into their modern equivalents, but did it as little as possible to preserve objectivity as well as the integrity of the author's intentions. Our adaptations represent less than 10% of the extracted keywords and allowed us to analyze four ancient texts (in addition to Ptolemy's) with the same method we analyzed the nine selected twentieth century textbooks. The following texts were selected:

> *Matheseos Libri VIII*, Firmicus Maternus (first publication, IV
> Century) *Le Commencement de la Sapience & le Livre
> des Fondements Astrologiques*, Abraham Ibn Ezra (first
> publication XII Century)
> *Traité des Jugements Généthliaques*, Henrich Rantzau (first
> publication, XVII Century)
> *Astrologiae Gallicae*, Jean-Baptiste Morin de Villefranche
> (first publication, XVII Century)

Together with Ptolemy's *Tetrabiblos* these ancient textbooks span fifteen centuries, from II AD to XVII AD. The results in Table VI are presented in the same format as those of the twentieth century textbooks in Table V, thereby facilitating comparisons between ancient and modern astrology.

The last two lines of Table VI give the percentages of coherencies obtained with the keywords of the five ancient textbooks and the nine modern textbooks. We can see that Saturn's symbolism is always the best described,

TABLE VI

Comparison of Five ancient astrologers'
keywords with our *typical lists*

N = Number of astrologers' keywords that are present in our traits catalogs
+ = Number of keywords that are in our *typical lists*
− = Number of keywords that are in the *opposed lists*
Mo, Ma, Ju, Sa =Number of keywords that belong to the *typical list* of another planet than the tested one.

Tested astrologer (chronological order)	MOON						MARS						JUPITER						SATURN						Percentage of coherencies
	N	+	−	Ma	Ju	Sa	N	+	−	Ma	Ju	Sa	N	+	−	Ma	Ju	Sa	N	+	−	Ma	Ju	Sa	
Ptolemy (IInd C.)	16	6	0	0	1	0	29	9.5	0	1	12	0	38	12	4	8	0	3	33	15.5	4	1	1	2	54%
Maternus (IV C.)	21	1	8	1	0	0	15	9	0	0	2	0	21	8	6	1	0	0	24	9	2	1	0	2	54%
Ibn Ezra (12 C.)	14	4	2	0	2	0	38	10	0	2	5	0	36	8	12	3	1	4	31	12	1	0	3	0	49%
Rantzau (17 C.)	13	4	2	0	0	0	24	6	0	0	10	0	23	6	4	4	0	1	37	13	4	0	1	3	50%
Morin de Villefranche (17 C.)	30	8	4	0	1	2	50	19	0	1	11	0	55	17	14	5	0	1	63	19	4	1	2	6	55%
Percentage of coherencies: 5 ancient astr.	50%						55%						42%						64%						53%
Percentage of coherencies: 9 modern astr.	71%						66%						60%						75%						68%

and Jupiter's least. The coherencies improve from the five ancient to the nine modern astrologers, favoring the hypothesis of a progressive improvement of astrological traditions through constant observation.

However, the percentages in the last column of Table VI refute our expectations: no improvement from the first to the last ancient text. Ptolemy's percentage of coherencies is as good as that of Morin de Villefranche, although there is a difference of fifteen centuries between their writings. Percentages from the medieval period writings of Ibn Ezra and Rantzau, are as low as chance expectations, with 49% and 50% coherencies respectively. Neither of these results supports our thesis.

On the one hand, the competency of the astrologers must be questioned, and not only the epoch in which they learned their craft. Which of these is more important is debatable.

On the other hand, the more contemporary language of recent astrologers may favor the comparison with our trait catalogs. The problem of the origin of planetary symbolism remains unsolved. Is the answer perhaps hidden in the numerous undeciphered clay tablets written by the first astrologers in Chaldea?

Chapter 9

THE MOST COMMON TRAIT WORDS

The astrologers' keywords give excellent results with some bodies of the solar system. With others, the results are uncertain or decidedly against astrological tradition. What, then, had to be our next step? Wouldn't it be logical to try to identify which, among the listed keywords, provide the most significant outcome?

We knew that some of the traits from our catalogs were used by the biographers of our notables only once, twice or three times, and others, hundreds of times. The most often quoted traits form statistically valid groups in and of themselves. We therefore proceeded to analyze each trait separately to determine which planet(s) produced positive and negative results in each case. Subsequently, we compared these results to the predictions made by the astrologers who mentioned it in their keywords for a particular planet. For example, if an astrologer wrote that *shy* is a Moon keyword, we checked the Moon's significance for this quoted trait. If another author had written that *shy* is a Saturn keyword, we compared both assertions with the results and decided which astrologer was right.

The results of an isolated trait are better ascertained if they are based on many data. Therefore, our first intention was to limit our study to the traits with at least one hundred data. However, the results from this analysis proved so interesting that we extended the limit to traits with 50 or more data.[1]

How the Isolated Traits Scored

Table VII lists the 253 separately analyzed traits. The number of birth data analyzed for a trait is listed after the name of the trait, followed by the planet(s) that yielded a significant result in that group of data. Only the positive results are listed in order to avoid confusion with **plus**, **minus**, **predicted** and **not predicted** results. Those results that were significantly negative are listed in Table IX. The remainder of each line is devoted to the planetary prediction in each studied textbook.[2]

---

[1]This limit was chosen by John Addey in his research published in "Harmonic Phase and Personal Characteristics," *The Astrological Journal, Summer 1979 & Winter 1979/80*, (1979-1980). Addey applied it to the French version of the catalogs. We chose to use, not only the traits that gathered 50 birth data or more in the French catalogs, but also those of the English translation of the catalogs, this being an objective criterion for increasing the number of analyzed data. (Often a single translation in English has been adopted for several French traits with the same meaning.)

[2]The textbook's predictions published in Table VII are restricted to the five (cont. on p.56)

TABLE VII
LIST OF THE ISOLATED TRAITS

First column: Traits that gather 50 birth data or more in our four catalogs, with the French and the English version added, listed in the English alphabetical order.

Second column: Number of birth data analyzed for the trait.

Third column: Positive results, at the 0.01 level significance, obtained after the rise and culmination (i.e. in *plus zones* or in *sectors 1+4*) for the Moon (L), Venus (V), Mars (M), Jupiter (J) and Saturn (S).

Last ten columns: Planet predicted in the ten studied astrological textbooks, in their paragraph about the five planets that gave results in our research: Moon (L), Venus (V), Mars (M), Jupiter (J), Saturn (S).

CHARACTER TRAIT	NUMBER OF CASES	SIGNIF. AFTER RISE & CULM.	PLANET PREDICTED BY THE STUDIED ASTROLOGERS									
			Ptolemy	Carter	Hone	Barbault	Hall	Mayo	Lee	Grell	Weingarten	Mann
Abundant	103	J+	J				J					
Active	357	M+		M	M		M	M		M,J	M	
Admirable	64	J+										
Affable	65		V			V						
Affectionate	67	J+		L,V	V		V	L,V	V		V	V
Ambitious	97	S+				S	M			J	S	
Amiable	146											
Amusing	58											
Animates others	182	M+										
Ardent	345	M+					M					M
Asserts himself	62			M,J	M	J		M		M		
Attentive	65											
Audacious	114	M+										
Authoritative	219	J+				J	M,J,S					S

CHARACTER TRAIT	NUMBER OF CASES	SIGNIF. AFTER RISE & CULM.	PLANET PREDICTED BY THE STUDIED ASTROLOGERS									
			Ptolemy	Carter	Hone	Barbault	Hall	Mayo	Lee	Grell	Weingarten	Mann
Bad tempered	66											
Bantering	195	J+										
Benevolent	95	V+	V				L,J			J		
Bohemian	52	J+										
Bold	80	M+								M		
Brilliant, sparkling, bursting	212	J+										
Calm	163	S+				S						
Careful	70	S+	S	L	S				S	J		
Charitable	69	L+								V		
Charming	423	J+							S	S		
Chaste	83						S					
Chief, Leader	98	M+	J		M	M						
Choleric	92	L+	M									
Clear	140					S	S				S	S
Cold	88	S+	S		S		L,S					
Combative	171	M+			M	M	M			M		
Comic	166	L+										
Common sense	86	S+					J					
Conscientious	303	S+										
Correct	52			L								
Countrylife, likes	73			M								
Courageous	376	M+	M		M	M	M		M	M	M	

CHARACTER TRAIT	NUMBER OF CASES	SIGNIF. AFTER RISE & CULM.	PLANET PREDICTED BY THE STUDIED ASTROLOGERS									
			Ptolemy	Carter	Hone	Barbault	Hall	Mayo	Lee	Grell	Weingarten	Mann
Courteous	74		V							V		
Creative	97											
Critical sense	165					M	J	V		L,V		
Cultivated	76											
Dandy	57	V+, J+										
Deep	98	S+	S			S						
Delicate	106											
Detached	70											
Devoted	199									V,M		
Dignified	104	S+						M,J,S		J		
Diligent	62											
Director	142	M+										
Direct	59				M						M	
Discreet	154	S+										
Disquiet	90											
Distant	60	S+										
Distinguished	129			V								
Dreamer, dreaming	181	L+, V+				L				L		
Dynamic	77	M+					M			M		
Ease, with	97	J+									V	
Eccentric	71	L+										
Efficacious	65	M+										
Elegant	208					V						

CHARACTER TRAIT	NUMBER OF CASES	SIGNIF. AFTER RISE & CULM.	PLANET PREDICTED BY THE STUDIED ASTROLOGERS									
			Ptolemy	Carter	Hone	Barbault	Hall	Mayo	Lee	Grell	Weingarten	Mann
Eloquent	52		V									
Energetic	258	M+		M,J	M	M	M	M	M	M	M	
Enthusiastic	220	V+		M,J			M			M		
Erudite	54	V+				S						
Esteemed	76	S+										
Exacting	70			M,J			M			S		
Excessive	57						S			J	J	
Experimenter	53	S+										
Expressive	55	J+								M		
Facility, has	68	L+,V+				V	S		J	S		
Faithful	242					S						
Fame, has tasted	63	V+						L				L
Family, likes	191	S+		L		L	L					
Famous	64											
Fervent	193											
Fiery	93			M								
Fighter, fighting	118			M	M	M		M			M	M
Financially, not motivated	181	M+,S+					S					
Firm	68											
Founder	105		J									
Frank	182					M			L,M			
Fraternal	50											
Freshness	61											

CHARACTER TRAIT	NUMBER OF CASES	SIGNIF. AFTER RISE & CULM.	PLANET PREDICTED BY THE STUDIED ASTROLOGERS									
			Ptolemy	Carter	Hone	Barbault	Hall	Mayo	Lee	Grell	Weingarten	Mann
Friendships, keeps	357		V				V,J,S,		V			V
Fun, fantasy, funny	275	L+, J+										
Gay (merry)	235	L+, J+	L,M	J	J	V	J			M,J	J	J
Generous	254	L+	V									
Good	362	S+										
Good comrade	55											
Good fellow	79	'S+										
Good-natured	81											
Good taste	83											
Good tempered, good mood	108	J+									V	
Gracious	161	V+	V		V	V	V					
Greathearted	156	V+										
Great beauty	52	V+, M+										
Group, in a	63	L+, M+										
Hard	93	M+		S		M		S				
Hardworking	474	S+				S						
Harsh	51	J+					L					
Haughty	52											
Heroic	56	M+								M	J	M
Honest	118					J	J					
Honored	150		V						J			

CHARACTER TRAIT	NUMBER OF CASES	SIGNIF. AFTER RISE & CULM.	PLANET PREDICTED BY THE STUDIED ASTROLOGERS									
			Ptolemy	Carter	Hone	Barbault	Hall	Mayo	Lee	Grell	Weingarten	Mann
Human	117											
Humble	58	L+										
Humorous	263		J				L,J			J, S		
Idealist	66	M+		V,M,J			L,J			J		
Imaginative	189			L	L	L	L,V			L		
Impetuous	62	J+					M					
Indefatigable	104											S
Independent	179						M			M		
Indulgent	71									V		
Influences others	112	V+,J+										
Innovator	52	S+										
Intellectual	104	S+										
Intelligent	394											
Intransigent	59	V+				S						
Ironic	174	J+		J			M					
Kind	163						L,V,J		L,J			
Laborious	133		S					S	S			
Laughing	105											
Lecturer	62			M								
Liberty, love of, free, freedom	91	L+										
Lightness	58	L+										
Literary writings	111											
Lively	246	M+,J+										

CHARACTER TRAIT	NUMBER OF CASES	SIGNIF. AFTER RISE & CULM.	PLANET PREDICTED BY THE STUDIED ASTROLOGERS									
			Ptolemy	Carter	Hone	Barbault	Hall	Mayo	Lee	Grell	Weingarten	Mann
Love, in	68	V+	V	V	V	V	V	V		V	V	V
Loved	175		V	V	V		V			V	V	V
Loyal	80			J								
Lucid	146											
Lyrical	136	L+				S						
Mastership	50	J+										
Measured, temperature	65		L,V,J				J					
Meditative	52	S+				S				S	S	J
Melancholy	65		S									S
Merry	128	J+	V			V						
Methodical	91	S+										
Middle class life, bourgeois	57										S	
Minute, attends to details	103	S+							L			
Modest	478	S+					L					
Mordant	61	J+										
Moving	87											
Mystic	60	L+										
Naive	83	L+										
Natural	167											
Nature, loves	57	L+	V									
Neat	64											

CHARACTER TRAIT	NUMBER OF CASES	SIGNIF. AFTER RISE & CULM.	PLANET PREDICTED BY THE STUDIED ASTROLOGERS									
			Ptolemy	Carter	Hone	Barbault	Hall	Mayo	Lee	Grell	Weingarten	Mann
Nervous	66								S			
Obliging	61											
Observant	163	S+										
Open	66		L						L	S		
Optimistic	73			J	J	J	L,J	J		J	J	J
Orderly	51			J		J	J,S	J			J	
Organizer	112					J					S	
Original	283	J+								V		
Passionate	364				M	M	M	M	M	M	M	
Passion for his art	91											
Patient	122	S+		S	S	S	J,S	S		S	S	
Patriotic	83							L				
Pedagogue	96	S+										
Penetrating	54						M		J			
Personality	490	J+				S	S					
Pessimistic	56					S	S			S		
Philosopher	89			J		S				J		J
Picturesque	102			J								
Poet	135	L+,J+					V					
Poor	61	L+,S+	S			L	S					
Popular	231	J+				J	L,J			J		
Powerful	225	J+					S	M,J				
Precise	175	S+										

CHARACTER TRAIT	NUMBER OF CASES	SIGNIF. AFTER RISE & CULM.	PLANET PREDICTED BY THE STUDIED ASTROLOGERS									
			Ptolemy	Carter	Hone	Barbault	Hall	Mayo	Lee	Grell	Weingarten	Mann
President	55											
Proud, pride	223	S+	J	L,S		S	J,S					
Prudent	69	S+	J									
Pure	72											
Quiet hobby	88											
Reads much	63	M+				J,S						
Realistic	74							S		M		
Rebellious	70							S				
Reflective	81	S+				S	J		L,S		L	L
Regular	75	L+,M+	V,J			J	J	S				
Religious	66	S+				S	S	J	J	J		J
Reserved	141	S+					S					S
Research worker	90						J					
Resolute	50	M+										
Respectful	51	S+										
Retirement	120	S+										
Rigorous	84											
Romantic	69					S	L			L,V		V
Rough	89			M			M					
Sad	77			S					S			
Scandalous	53	V+	S	J			S					
Scientific	118		J				S					
Scrupulous	97	S+										
Secretive	85	S+					M,S			S		

CHARACTER TRAIT	NUMBER OF CASES	SIGNIF. AFTER RISE & CULM.	PLANET PREDICTED BY THE STUDIED ASTROLOGERS									
			Ptolemy	Carter	Hone	Barbault	Hall	Mayo	Lee	Grell	Weingarten	Mann
Seductive	113											
Seeks the truth	65											
Self-willed	333	M+,J+		L	L	L,V	M			M	L	
Sensitive	360				M	V	V	V	V,M	L,V,S	M	L
Sensual	76											
Sentimental	75	L+		L			V					
Serene	55	S+						V				
Serious	112				S	S		S		S	S	S
Severe	64	S+			S					S		
Sharp	53	S+				M	M					
Silent	91	S+								S		
Simple	647											
Sincere	220								J	S	S	
Skillful	81											
Smiling	208	J+				V						
Sober	119											
Sociable	55			V,M,J					V	L,V		V
Soft	198					V	L,V	V	V			
Solemn, grave	89	S+		S								
Solid	79					S						
Solitary	224	S+	S									
Sparkling	78	J+		J	J	J						
Spontaneous	92											
Sporting	70	J+										

CHARACTER TRAIT	NUMBER OF CASES	SIGNIF. AFTER RISE & CULM.	Ptolemy	Carter	Hone	Barbault	Hall	Mayo	Lee	Grell	Weingarten	Mann
						PLANET PREDICTED BY THE STUDIED ASTROLOGERS						
Steadfast	127	S+						V				
Straight	112											
Strength, full of	134					M	L,M,V	M			M	M
Strenuous	68											
Stubborn, persistent	113	M+	L									
Subtle	285		V									
Successful	197	V+,J+			J	J	J			J		
Supple	66											
Susceptible to influence	57	L+				L						
Sympathetic	230	J+		L,J			L,J	V	V			
Talkative, garrulous	102	S+										
Teaches	65											J
Technician	63						S					M
Tenacious	141	M+		L	L		S					
Tender	156					V	S					
Timid	209	S+	L,V,J	L			S		S			
Tranquil	76											
Traveller	224	V+				L	L					
True	67											
Trustworthy, sure	92	S+										
Unsociable	77	S+										

CHARACTER TRAIT	NUMBER OF CASES	SIGNIF. AFTER RISE & CULM.	PLANET PREDICTED BY THE STUDIED ASTROLOGERS									
			Ptolemy	Carter	Hone	Barbault	Hall	Mayo	Lee	Grell	Weingarten	Mann
Upright	96											
Varied	59		L	L								
Verve	224	J+										
Vibrating	53											
Vigorous	73	M+	M,S									
Violent	110					M	M			M	M	
Vitality	94	M+,J+				J	M					
Warm	53	J+		M,J		J	V,J	V,M				J
Welcoming	56											
Wise, segacious	133	L+,J+				S	J		S	S		J
Witty, witticism	405	L+		S								M
Worldly	79					V						
Youthful	164	L+,V+				V						
Zealous	50											

The following is an example of the data from Table VIII, and their interpretation:

Abundant   103   J +   (Pt) J   (Ha) J

Abundant: The trait *abundant* was attributed to 103 notables by their biographers as a description of their gestures, writings, speeches, etc.
103:   The birth moments of these 103 notables were analyzed.
J +:   They produced a **significantly** positive result for Jupiter.
(Pt) J: Ptolemy mentions *abundant* as a keyword for Jupiter.
(Ha) J: Hall also mentions *abundant* as a keyword for Jupiter.

These two authors were correct in predicting a relationship between the extroverted trait *abundant* and the planet Jupiter. Their predictions are confirmed by the birth data of the 103 notables described as having this trait. The other studied astrologers did not mention *abundant* among their keywords for Jupiter. Thus, their column remains empty on this line.

The second trait, *active*, was analyzed with 357 birth data. These produced a significant number of Mars positions in **plus zones** indicated by **M +** . This trait is correctly predicted as typical for Mars by six astrologers: Carter, Hone, Hall, Mayo, Grell and Weingarten.

The third trait, *admirable*, with 64 birth data, produced a significant number of Jupiter positions in **plus zones** indicated by **J +** . Interestingly enough, none of the consulted textbooks mentions it as a keyword for Jupiter.

On the next two lines the trait *affable*, predicted by two astrologers as positive for Venus, and the trait *affectionate*, predicted as positive for Venus and the Moon by seven astrologers, respectively, do not reach the 0.01 level of significance. This lack of statistical confirmation does not necessarily discount the astrologers' predictions. These samples are small, only 65 and 67 cases, and thus do not easily render significant results even if the effect exists. After checking our files we stated that the predicted planets gave a slightly positive result. If the samples were increased, the predictions of the astrologers might be confirmed.

The rest of Table VII can be interpreted as described above. Some of the results are quite in agreement with the astrologers' predictions, others less so, and still others are contradictory. For instance, the trait *ambitious*

(cont. from p. 43) significant bodies Moon, Venus, Mars, Jupiter and Saturn. The predictions concerning the five non significant bodies are not mentioned here, in order not to overload the Table, even though all the ten bodies were studied in the same way. Again the Sun, Mercury, Uranus, Neptune and Pluto failed to yield results, except in a few odd cases; like the keywords *Comic* and *Dreamer* giving a positive Sun result; the keywords *Clear* or *Welcoming* giving a positive Pluto result. . . . Their scarcity and psychological incoherence make us consider such results as accidental fluctuations, related to astronomical or demographic peculiarities of the studied groups.

is considered a Saturn keyword by Barbault and Weingarten; but the results are significant for Jupiter, as Grell predicted. Grell attributes the trait *charitable* to Jupiter but the result is significant for the Moon.

An attentive examination of Table VII leads to the conclusion that an opinion given by only one astrologer is most often contradicted by the results. When more than one astrologer agree on a trait attributed to a planet, their choice is most often confirmed by the results. However, the keywords *generous* and *religious*, ascribed to Jupiter by six and seven astrologers, respectively, are two notable exceptions to this rule. In both cases the result appears to be significant with the Moon instead of Jupiter.

Thus, Table VII suggests some pertinent rectifications of various opinions about the planetary keywords.

Synthesis of Typical & Opposed Traits for Each Planet

A synthesized view of the range of influence of the Moon, Venus, Mars, Jupiter and Saturn is obtained by listing, under each planet, the significant isolates. Table VIII presents the list of positively significant isolates for the Moon, Venus, Mars, Jupiter and Saturn; Table IX, the opposite picture — the list of negatively significant isolates for the same bodies. There is no list of significant isolates for the remaining bodies (see note on page 52).

Some lists are longer and some shorter, but the differences in length are reflective only of the amount of linguistic data available, demonstrating, in degrees, the difficulty encountered in obtaining statistical results for these planetary traits.

What is important here is the truly objective description of the characteristic and antithetical personality traits linked to the Moon, Venus, Mars, Jupiter and Saturn. Such objective summaries may contain some surprises for traditional astrologers. For instance, the isolates present not Jupiter, but Venus as *benevolent* and *greathearted*; not Saturn but Jupiter as *harsh*, *ambitious*; and so forth.

However, we must not forget that some results were gathered from rather small samples of data and could still change with increased sets of character traits. It is our intention to improve the accuracy of the results by gathering new documents about personality traits and the planets, in the U.S. This search has already begun.

On the whole, the picture of each planet's characteristics offered by these lists of significant isolates seems coherent. It is particularly interesting to note both the positive and the negative side of the results for Jupiter, a planet that has shown so much variance with the astrologers' keywords. Here its main characteristics appear to be *extroversion, brilliance, liveliness* and *authority*. The Saturn personality that emerges from the significant isolates deserves some consideration for being more calm and peaceful than the traditional textbooks usually described. Even the description of the Moon reflected by the isolates contains some suggestions toward necessary

TABLE VIII

Synthesized Picture of Each Planet's Personality

The results are **positive** in plus zones (or sectors following rise and culmination) for the Moon, Venus, Mars, Jupiter and Saturn, with the following traits.*

MOON IS:	VENUS IS:	MARS IS:	JUPITER IS:	SATURN IS:
Charitable	Benevolent	Active	Abundant	Amiable
Choleric	Dandy	Animates	Admirable	Calm
Comic	Erudite	others	Ambitious	Careful
Dreamer	Facility, has	Ardent	Authority,	Cold
Facility, has	Gracious	Audacious	has	Common
Funny	Greathearted	Bold	Bantering	sense
Gay	Great beauty	Chief	Bohemian	Conscientious
Generous	Love, in	Combative	Brilliant	Deep
Group, in a	Scandalous	Courageous	Charming	Dignified
Humorous	Successful	Director	Dandy	Discreet
Lightness	Youthful	Dynamic	Ease, with	Distant
Loves		Efficacious	Expressive	Esteemed
freedom		Energetic	Gay (merry)	Experimenter
Loves nature		Hard	Harsh	Family, likes
Lyrical		Heroic	Impetuous	Financially
Mystic		Lively	Influences	motivated,
Naive		Realistic	others	not
Poet		Resolute	Ironic	Good
Religious		Self-willed	Liked	Good fellow
Sentimental		Stubborn	Lively	Hard
Susceptible		Tenacious	Mastership	working
to influences		Vigorous	Merry	Intellectual
Witty		Vitality	Mordant	Meditative
Worldly			Original	Methodical
Youthful			Personality	Minute
			Popular	Modest
			Powerful	Observant
			Self-willed	Patient
			Smiling	Pedagogue
			Sparkling	Poor
			Successful	Precise
			Verve	Prudent
			Vitality	Pure
			Warm	Reflective
			Witty	Reserved
				Research
				worker
				Respectful
				Retires
				Scrupulous
				Secretive
				Serene
				Severe
				Silent
				Simple
				Solemn
				Solitary
				Straight

*As with for the other bodies, here also one or two traits were so obviously in contradiction with the planet's symbolism that we considered them as statistical odds and left them out. Example: *Traveler* for Venus, *Great Beauty* for Mars.

Teaches
Timid
Trustworthy
Unsociable

TABLE IX

Synthesized Picture of Each Planet's Antipersonality

The results are **negative** in plus zones (or sectors following rise and culmination) for the Moon, Venus, Mars, Jupiter and Saturn, with the following traits.*

THE MOON IS NOT:	VENUS IS NOT:	MARS IS NOT:	JUPITER IS NOT:	SATURN IS NOT:
Ambitious	Common	Charming	Affectionate	Abundant
Animates	sense	Comic	Dignified	Amusing
others	Conscientious	Detached	Dreamer	Bantering
Ardent	Frank	Family life,	Faithful	Bohemian
Authority,	Good fellow	likes	Family life,	Combative
has	Mordant	Good taste	likes	Comic
Clear	Popular	Love, in	Financially	Dandy
Cold	Prudent	Loved	motivated,	Group, in a
Combative	Reserved	Picturesque	not	Humorous
Courageous	Retires	Poet	Generous	Facility, has
Courteous	Scrupulous	Sensitive	Good	Freedom,
Director	Seeks truth	Tranquil	Human	loves
Esteemed	Sporting	Witty	Humble	Funny
Exacting	Strength,	Youthful	Loves nature	Imaginative
Experimenter	full of		Mystic	Impetuous
Gracious	Teaches		Naive	Ironic
Hard	True		Poor	Lightness
working	Witty			
Influences				
others				
Intelligent				
Laborious				
Observant				
Organizer				
Passion for				
his art				
Pedagogue				
Penetrating				
Powerful				
Precise				
Scandalous				
Scientific				
Self-willed				
Steadfast				
Straight				
Tenacious				

*As with the other bodies, here also one or two traits were so obviously in contradiction with the planet's symbolism that we considered them as statistical odds and left them out. Example: *Traveler* for Venus, *Great Beauty* for Mars.

adaptations: *mystical sense*, for example, belongs to the realm of the Moon and not to Jupiter, as is usually suggested. Mars and Venus seem to be the bodies for which the traditional picture was most upheld, with no changes appearing necessary for them within the context of this synthesis.

Chapter 10

JUPITER'S REAL NATURE

Our first test with the planetary keywords showed that most textbooks do not provide a correct picture of Jupiter characteristics. The keywords attributed to Jupiter failed to produce any result in nine cases out of ten; and the Sun keywords produced results for Jupiter in six cases out of ten. Needless to say, the astrologers' planetary descriptions are incongruent in Jupiter's case.

In our second test, on the proportions of coherencies, it became clear that some of the astrologers' keywords for Jupiter describe real Jovian characteristics and thus, only a part of their keywords appeared to be erroneous. The next task was to identify the correct part of the descriptions.

In our third test, with the most often quoted traits from our catalogs, a coherent picture of the real Jovian characteristics began to emerge. Unfortunately, the lists of significant traits are still too small.

A much more detailed list of statistically well-ascertained Jupiter traits from the biographies of hundreds of successful actors has been published in our *Jupiter Temperament and Actors* (LERRCP Publications, 1974). In the present book (page 5), Table I presents the most relevant of these traits in order of their level of significance, i.e., *lively, verve, sparkling, personality, bantering, witty, abundant, ironic, good-tempered, original.* With these, the picture for Jupiter becomes consistent.

Upon scanning the 71 initially consulted textbooks, I noticed that most of the correct keywords appeared in the paragraph dedicated to the description of an "ill-aspected" Jupiter. Most errors fell in the descriptions of the "well-aspected" Jupiter. Let us test this new hypothesis for better identifying Jupiter's typical traits.

The Ill-Aspected Jupiter

Keywords contained in the relevant paragraphs were collected to test the astrologers' descriptions of an "ill-aspected" Jupiter. Although these paragraphs bore different titles, their meaning was always of a depreciatory nature, i.e., *dishonorable, bad, misused, negative* and so forth. Table X presents the keyword lists extracted from the negative keyword paragraphs of the studied textbooks.

All of these keywords were submitted to the rigors of our first test that calculated the number of Jupiter positions in **plus zones** for the moment of birth of the notables they described. Despite a drastic reduction in the number of data tested when compared to the total Jupiter descriptions

---

TABLE X

The Keywords Belonging to the Ill-Aspected Jupiter

Ptolemy: Jupiter "in a dishonorable position" is *arrogant, superstitious, timid, proud, negligent* and *embarrasses others*

Carter: The qualities of a "bad" Jupiter are *over optimism, waste, verbalism*

Hone: The "misused" Jupiter is *extremist, improvident, provocative, sporting, wasteful*

Barbault: (no description of the "ill-aspected" Jupiter)

Hall: A "negative" Jupiter is *extravagant, dissipated, conceited, fanatical, self-loving, not critical, irresolute, lazy*

Mayo: An "afflicted" Jupiter is *exaggerated, extravagant, conceited*

Lee: Jupiter, "not properly situated" is *extravagant, conceited, a gambler, hypocritical and fanatical.*

Grell: A "negative" Jupiter is *extravagant, excessive, fanatical, extremist, confiding in others, indolent, dissipated, conceited, pompous, ostentatious, and likes display*

Weingarten: The "minus" type of Jupiter is *extravagant, wasteful, a show-off, haughty, confiding in others, opportunistic, a gambler, hypocritical.*

Mann: (no description of the "ill-aspected" Jupiter)

(positive and negative) by the same astrologers, the keywords corresponding to the "ill-aspected" Jupiter produced a significantly positive result (P = 0.007). The hypothesis was confirmed: the so-called negative traits of the Jupiter descriptions contain most of the correct traditional keywords. Simultaneously, the "well-aspected" Jupiter descriptions contain most of the keywords that tradition erroneously attributes to this planet. The "bad" keywords are then the statistically good ones, and the "good" keywords, are the statistically inconclusive ones — a useful hint for understanding Jupiter's real characteristics.

Test Your Own Jupiter Image

You may have your own list of Jupiter characteristics or you may instead trust the Jupiter descriptions of one particular author. Wouldn't it be interesting to test them using the lists of Typical and Opposed Traits for Mars, Saturn, Jupiter and the Moon as published in our *Psychological Monographs*?[1]

The following will describe, taking Ptolemy's keyword list for Jupiter as an example, how this book may be used for testing and verifying your own keyword list.

---

[1]Collected in the "Scientific Document Number 1," *The Planetary Factors in Personality*. May be acquired from Laboratoire d'Etude des Relations entre Rhythmes Cosmiques et Psychophysiologiques, 8, rue Amyot, 75005, Paris, France.

Ptolemy's Jupiter Keywords: *temperate, overheated, beneficent, masculine, glory, abundant, likes rest, peaceful, superior manner, beneficent, liberal, glory, magnanimous, beneficent, religious, jolly, human, splendid, liberal, just, greatness, grave, prolific, prudent, loving, chief, greatness, arrogant, religious, superstitious, reserved, timid, majestic, proud, frank, embarrasses others, liberal, negligent.*

This list can be checked for keywords that are categorized in our *Psychological Monographs* as Typical and Opposed Traits for Mars, Jupiter, Saturn and the Moon. One could first check the Typical Traits for Jupiter and label each corresponding keyword as **Jupiter +** . The keywords appearing among the Opposed Traits for Jupiter should be labeled **Jupiter —** . **Moon +** will indicate a keyword that is neither present in the Typical Traits nor in the Opposed Traits list for Jupiter, but in the Typical Traits for the Moon. **Mars +** will indicate the presence of a keyword in the Typical Traits list for Mars; **Saturn +** , a presence in the Typical Traits for Saturn. Some neutral or unidentifiable traits will remain without notation after the completion of this task. Table XI presents, in separate columns, the various components of Ptolemy's Jupiter keyword lists.[2]

The columns of Table XI clearly show Ptolemy's concept of Jupiter's realm of influence, compared to what our statistical tests have revealed. The keywords *greatness, splendid, majestic* all belong to one central part of the Jovian personality, together with its exaggerations, *superior* and *proud*. *Jolly* belongs to another typical part of this personality; *frank* describes yet another less known aspect of this way of being; *chief* and *glory* are the frequent consequences in life of possessing the above mentioned Jovian traits.

Other features of the Ptolemy's description of Jupiter are erroneous. He describes the Jovian type as middle aged, calm, even bourgeois, as reflected in his keywords: *likes rest, peaceful, human, grave*. However, these keywords have been proven to belong to the opposed personality: Jupiter gives significantly negative results in **plus zones** with these words.

This false idea of Jupiter as a calm, kind being is further emphasized by keywords belonging to the Moon personality. Such Moon keywords are: *loving, liberal, temperate* and their weakness, *negligent*. Ptolemy attributes two other important Moon keywords, *religious* and *prolific* (and their various synonyms), to Jupiter.

Some of Ptolemy's Jupiter keywords even belong to the Saturn personality: *just, prudent, timid, reserved*.[3] It does not appear that these traits would be considered Jupiterian nowadays.

[2]Excerpts from Nicolas Bourdin's French translation of the *Tetrabiblos* of Ptolemy. Astrologers having suggested that we should rather analyze F.E. Robbins' English translation, we asked Thomas Shanks to do this analysis on ACS's computer. The results are worse for Jupiter. So we published our French selection of keywords (results given in Figure 4, p. 18).

TABLE XI

Among Ptolemy's Jupiter keywords the following ones are statistically proven to belong to:

Jupiter +	Jupiter −	Moon +	Saturn +
Glory	Likes	Temperate	Just
Abundant	rest	Liberal	Prudent
Superior	Peaceful	Religious	Timid
manners	Human	Prolific	Reserved
Jolly	Grave	Loving	
Splendid		Negligent	
Greatness			
Chief			
Majestic			
Proud			
Frank			

However, we can say that, on the whole, the astrologer has perceived the extroverted qualities of the Jupiter personality. Actually, the main problem is that the quality of extroversion has hard and soft aspects. Only the hard part belongs to Jupiter, as our inquiry with the "ill-aspected" Jupiter has shown (see pages 61-62). The soft side of extroversion seems to belong to the Moon. In our opinion, the present analysis of Ptolemy's keywords presents a good illustration of this principle.

Now, the question turns to you. What is **your** description of Jupiter? What is **your** analysis of the Moon? We recommend that you study these planets as above, if you are inclined to accept some degree of change in your opinions.

[3]In Robbin's English translation of the *Tetrabiblos*, the Jupiter keywords contain more Saturn traits. This explains the significantly negative results for Jupiter's positions in *plus zones* mentioned in Chapter 4, footnote 1. Furthermore, a significantly positive Saturn result appeared with the Jupiter keywords. A real pole inversion!

Chapter 11

CONCLUSION

What shall we conclude?

First, of course, my rational position as a scientist has been shaken by the numerous significant results obtained with the astrological keywords for the Moon, Venus, Mars and Saturn. A link exists between some planetary positions at birth as conveyed by traditional books, and the native's personality. However, the link is not of the exact nature that these textbooks would have us understand. The planetary positions **are not dominant before** the horizon and meridian axes (Houses I and X) but **are dominant after** them (sectors 1, 4, 7, 10). Furthermore, a correspondence could not be established for all the bodies as predicted by the astrologers. The Sun never yielded a result. Mercury, Uranus, Neptune and Pluto did not achieve significant results by themselves, and require further investigation.

Nevertheless, there is more to the old Chaldean soothsayers' lore than a rationalist would expect. The idea that cosmic forces have an influence on human affairs appears to hold some fundamental truth — a reality hard for me to admit. My opinions were uprooted even more by the realization that this link is not of a general, comprehensive nature, but produced from exact predictions of the consulted textbooks. The planets are related to the human personality, and this relationship shows up at the moment of birth. Very strange indeed!

Even so, with large quantities of data, we have proven that the link is not as consistant as astrologers would have us believe. The planet does not directly influence the native's future by molding the infant's character when the birth takes place. If all goes well, the fetus chooses the moment of its birth as if this would be programmed by the temperament it has inherited from its parents. The infant seems to be sensitive to the position of a specific planet after rise and culmination and induces its own delivery when the stars are in a position corresponding to its genes. This was proven through the study of thousands of family data (see our *Series B*) although it was not predicted by the textbooks.

It is the link with the character traits that was predicted with great accuracy, as well as the type of character which is effectively related to the Moon, Venus, Mars and Saturn. This surprised me the most.

Still, many puzzling problems remain unsolved. Why did the Sun fail to give results with the astrologers' keywords? Could it be because the Sun is not a planet but the star of our solar system? Why did Mercury fail to produce the predicted results? Because it is too small to have an effect on the Earth? What of the distant planets Uranus, Neptune and Pluto? Are they too remote to produce an effect, or are recent occultists less intuitive than ancient astrologers who described the heavenly bodies known in their time? If so, why then, do we find better results with the keywords of the modern rather than the ancient astrologers? Is it due to language differences or do crucial differences exist?

The case of Jupiter, the worst guess of the ancients, shows seemingly better interpretation by the more recent practitioners. Do these more recent practitioners progressively better their intuition by observation of their clients' reactions? Why were such intuitions not powerful enough to put the emphasis on astronomically correct, dominant sectors of the charts — the regions situated **after** and **not before** the horizon and meridian axes?

We can take a look at the way in which this intuition may have worked by reading chart interpretations in the astrological literature. For instance, in *Profiles of Women* (AFA 1979), Lois Rodden lists 500 birth data to illustrate "the female role as played through the twelve signs of the zodiac." Rodden has chosen the zodiac signs as the criterion for classifying her data. Here and there in her chart interpretations, she mentions the Sun sign under which a woman was born, as a factor in her character or in the events of her life, a practice natural with such a classification system.

However, in our research we never obtained results with Sun sign classifications. Therefore, I remain skeptical when I read allusions which I would describe as farfetched and that are imposed by the chosen classification rather than by clear events or traits.

Lois Rodden uses many other astronomical features in her interpretation of charts. Among them, and of most interest to me, are the planetary positions in Houses XII or IX. These **cadent** houses are **weak** and **uninteresting**, according to astrological tradition. Yet, in our research they are the principal sectors that reveal strong characters and successful professionals. How does Lois Rodden interpret such cases?

In one case out of two, her interpretation ignores the planet occupying such an astrologically uninteresting place. In the other half of the cases, she stresses its proximity to the axes. This dual method of interpretation interests me. Without traditional support indicating the effect of planets situated after their rise or culmination, Lois Rodden nonetheless, one out of two times, describes this planetary phenomenon and mentions it as positive. Doesn't this show that her unconscious mind provided some realistic intuition?

A good example of the above appears in her analysis of the chart of Sylvia Kars, a medical assistant who became a "sensuality therapist." The planets situated after the meridian and horizon axes in this chart are not considered important in one segment of the description, but are used to explain the subject's reactions in a later description. Let me refer to the two relevant paragraphs.

Paragraph 1 — *No Correct Intuition at Work*

Rodden quotes her Libra subject, Kars, describing her own personality: "I always felt that I was **helping** others. There was a **close, caring, nurturing interaction** with my clients." Rodden further writes of Kars' **natural speaking ability,** noting that Kars has fulfilled hundreds of speaking engagements in her work: extended coverage on **radio** and **television**, in **magazines** and **workshops** and the **writing of a book**. All of the above keywords emphasized in bold, have been shown to be typical of the Moon in our inquiries. Effectively, if we look at the position of the Moon in Sylvia Kars' chart, we find it in House XII, our sector 1, one of the two key sectors in our results.

But astrological tradition does not consider House XII as meaningful for the personality, and Lois Rodden ignores this Moon position, mentioning Saturn in House I, Uranus in House II, Neptune in House VII and Pluto in House VI to explain her subject's personality. My individual opinion is that there is no link between Kars' personality and these planets; not any more than with the Sun sign Libra.

Paragraph 2 — Correct Intuition at Work

I felt much more convinced as I read the planetary allusions to Venus and Mars in Scorpio to explain Kars' pioneering work in **sexual rehabilitation** as a surrogate **sex partner** for eight to ten clients per week; a leader of a subcultural movement of nude **sexuality** classes; and a slender, tanned **tennis buff**. These planets have been proven to relate to these character traits, emphasized in bold. These planets are situated in House IX (our sector 4). Sensuality and Venus, sports and Mars, and their positions in the chart perfectly correspond to our results. Only the Sun in Scorpio seems extraneous or irrelevant.

Why does the importance of Venus and Mars after the Midheaven **not** escape Lois Rodden while she fails to recognize the position of the Moon after the Ascendant? To me, the keywords in Sylvia Kars' biographical notes are as clear in the first case as in the second, and the Moon is nearer to the Ascendant (4°) than Venus and Mars to the Midheaven (6° and 13°, respectively).

This is one example of the way in which the astrologers' intuition may work. Among the extremely numerous factors they learn to interpret in a chart, they pick out this or that factor and relate it to the biographical traits, sometimes correctly and sometimes incorrectly.

Throughout the centuries, this method of trial and error, together with their clients' behavior, may have guided the astrologers toward a partial knowledge of what the statistical methods have revealed to us: **the planetary positions after the horizon and meridian axes are related in a still mysterious way to our personality and behavior**. Without this partial knowledge of the astrologers, the statistical methods would never have been applied to this particular field. For this reason, astrological intuition is now something I value considerably more.

APPENDIX

Introduction to the Appendix

The new statistical results described in this book are based on the keywords from the chapter describing the planets in each of the ten following astrological textbooks, listed chronologically:

> *Tetrabiblos*, Ptolemy, C. (first publication Second Century AD)
> *The Principles of Astrology*, Carter, C.E.O. (first publication 1925)
> *The Modern Textbook of Astrology*, Hone, M. (first publication 1951)
> *Défense et Illustration de l'Astrologie*, Barbault, A. (1955)
> *Astrological Keywords*, Hall, M. P. (first publication 1958)
> *Teach Yourself Astrology*, Mayo, J. (1964)
> *Dictionary of Astrology*, Lee, D. (1968)
> *Keywords*, Grell, P. (1970)
> *The Study of Astrology*, Weingarten, H. (1977)
> *The Round Art*, Mann, A.T. (1978)

Researchers may wish to control the objectivity of our method by checking these keywords in the relevant chapters. Others may want to attempt new research. Not all that can be done has been done. We hope that our readers will apply their hypotheses to our material. Students of astrology may also be interested in the synthesis of each noted astrologer's opinion about the planets, as reflected in the keyword lists.

The complete lists of keywords for each author are published in this Appendix. Their exact succession has been maintained, even the repetitions of some traits, to facilitate their identification throughout the relevant texts. These repetitions reflect those qualities the authors seem to emphasize as typical of each planet.

Since the first thing that one tends to want to do with this document is compare the descriptions of one particular planet across authors, we adopt this grouping of the keywords.

The ten heavenly bodies are listed in the order adopted by the ten textbooks: the Sun, the Moon, Mercury, Venus, Mars, Jupiter, Saturn, Uranus, Neptune and Pluto. Under the name of each planet, the keywords of each author appear in chronological order of the publication date of their texts:

> Ptolemy (II AD), Carter (1925), Hone (1951), Barbault (1955), Hall (1958), Mayo (1964), Lee (1968), Grell (1970), Weingarten (1977), and Mann (1978).

With this succession of data, one can easily check hypotheses about the evolution of astrological ideas through time. At first glance, the various keyword lists for each body show a great variety of traits. For instance, the keyword lists for the Sun includes:

> **Ptolemy** — *just, religious, grave*
> **Carter** — *positive, strong, vigorous*
> **Barbault** — *alive, warm, bright*

There is no linguistic or psychological link between these terms. Does this impede astrological correlations? Not at all. Despite the stated absence of Sun results with Sun keywords (as described in this volume), some coherent results appear with the Sun keywords for Jupiter and Mars. The link is not apparent, but lies hidden in the various words.

A great deal of further statistical work is needed to consolidate the results obtained from these keyword lists. We feel pleased that others might want to carry on this work.

THE KEYWORDS FOR
EACH PLANET IN THE TEN
ASTROLOGICAL TEXTBOOKS

SUN KEYWORDS

Ptolemy
Just
Religious
Grave
Difficulties, has
Persistent
Rough
Cruel
Stiff-necked

Noisy
Loud
Quarrelsome
Vain
Warm
Spirit
Idealistic
Enthusiastic
Timid, not
Sociable

Carter
Positive
Strong
Vigorous
Dignified
Abundant
Affectionate
Helpful
Leader
Virile
Buoyant
Magnanimous
Open
Ostentatious
Bombastic
Sensualistic
Sentimental
Selfish
Self-confidence
Vitality
Personality
Leader
Bombast
Bluffer
Exuberant
Aggressive
Asserts himself

Hone
Powerful
Vitality
Creative
Personality
Expressive
Dignified
Domineering
Faithful
Gay (Merry)
Organizer
Magnanimous
Proud
Royal
Affectionate
Arrogant
Autocratic
Changing, not
Childish
Playful
Condescending
Despot
Extravagant
Gushing
Pompous

Barbault
Alive
Warm
Bright
Radiant
Strength
Youthful
High conscience
Conscientious
Idealist
Self-willed
Logical
Virile
Vocation
Mastership
Heroic
Proud
Magnanimous
Aristocratic
Powerful
Generous
Open
Educator
Professor
Patron
Chief
King
Authority
Guide
Heroic
Cultivated
Sociable
Spectacular
Social action
Dignified
Honors, likes
Successful
Renowned
Elevation
Power, has
Grand
Heroic
Ostentatious
Theatrical
Socialist

Hall
Virile
Vigorous
Perfect
Hot
Dry
Powerful
Accomplished
Restless
Emotional
Dignified
Patron
Paternal
Ambitious
Organizer
Wise
Counselor
Strong
Generous
Master
Honest
Creative
Vitality
Constructive
Educator
Ostentatious
Ambitious, not
Pompous
Despot
Formal
Ceremonious
Consciousness
Authority
Responsibility
Leader
Goldsmith
Success
Public man
Fame
Healthy

Excessive
Rich
Noble
Honorary
  distinction
Reformer
King
President
Fortune
Honor
Esteemed
Individuality

Mayo
Power
Individualistic
Conscious
Complete
Spiritual
Creative
Authority
Energetic
Vitality
Equilibrated

Lee
Individualistic
Creative
Leader
Noble
Sincere
Proud
Ambitious
Intense
Show-off
Despotic
Ceremonious

Grell
Giver
Spiritualism
Energetic
Self-willed

Ambitious
Self-conscious
Strength, full of
Authority
Individualistic
Vitality
Leader
Confident
Bold
Determined
Honors
Faithful
Stable
Loyal
Dignified
Grateful
Zealous
Generous
Arrogant
Rebel
Austere
Indolent
Vain
Despot
Ostentatious
Dictatorial
Bluntness
  of speech
Luxury, likes
Contemptuous
Jealous

Weingarten
Vitality
Self-willed
Power, has
Leader
Dignified
Character, has
Egocentric
Assertive
Desires
Authoritative

Famous
Proud
Arrogant
Appreciated
Applauded
Egocentric
Domineering

Mann
Spirituality
Paternal
Leader
Active
Self willed
Energetic

Vitality
Organizer
Power, has
Creative
King
Official
Objective
Conscious
Rational
Energy
Flame
Heroic
Assertive

MOON KEYWORDS

Ptolemy
Flabby
Overheated
Beneficent
Temperate
Femininity
Noctambulist
Varied
Subtle
Inconstant
Generous
Open-minded
Assured
Free
Coward
Timid
Abject

Carter
Feminine
Receptive
Imaginative
Careful
Prudent
Timid
Domesticated
Shrewd
Practical
Maternal
Affectionate
Sympathetic
Impressionable
Emotional
Changeable
Tenacious
Past, likes the

Passive
Prejudiced
Narrow
Home loving
Family, likes
Morbid
Sensitive
Self-conscious
Fluctuating
Varied
Receptive
Protector
Home, likes
Country, likes
Sentimental

Hone

Fluctuations
Changing
Feminine
Imaginative
Maternal
Protector
Receptive
Sensitive
Tenacious
Reasonable, not
Fussy
Invert
Touchy

Barbault

Prolific
Childish
Unconscious,
   importance of
Infantile
Maternal
Imagination
Dreamer
Memory, good
Delirious
Folkloric

Mythology,
   interest in
Sensitive
Emotional
Impressionable
Influence,
   susceptible to
Dependent
Imaginative
Dreaming
Capricious
Poet
Inconstant
Lazy
Weak
Egocentric
Narcissistic
Feminine
Queen
Children, likes
Animals, likes
Home, likes his
Family, likes
Travel, fond of
Childish
Primitive
Lower class
Fashionable
Republican
Poetical
Narrator
Fabling
Keeps a diary
Anecdotes, tells
Folklore, likes

Hall

Cold
Feminine
Heavy
Soft
Dark
Gloomy

Bright
Optimistic
Concentrated, not
Imaginative
Instinctive
Imagination
Family, likes
Home loving
Human
Receptive
Intuitive
Magnetism
Positive
Peaceful
Ingenious
Maternal
Travel, fond of
Visionary
Frivolous
Mediumistic
Capricious
Interesting, not
Lazy
Conscious
Harmonious
Magnetic
Sea, likes the
Traveller
Children, likes
Mysteries
Romantic
Idealistic
Fanciful
Popularity
Inhibited
Emotional
Public man
Responsibilities,
  assumes
Changes
Emotional
Apathetic
Antipathies, has

Depression
Fluidity
Domesticated
Popularity
Honest
Physical strength
Hope
Faith
Venerates others
Benevolent
Imitator
Sympathetic
Suave
Kind
Modest
Animals, loves
Protector
Defends others
Maternal

Mayo
Instinctive
Evolves
Conscious
Unconsciousness
Maternal
Emotional
Affectionate
Desires
Disturbed
Lunatics
Past, likes the
Sensations,
  open to
Restless
Changeable
Family, likes
Patriotic

Lee
Reflective
Impressionable
Changeable
Frank

Open
Refined
Kind
Modest
Visionary
Lazy
Frivolous

Grell
Spiritualism
Imaginative
Creative
Femininity
Formal
Negative
Maternal
Changeable
Sensitive
Receptive
Instinctive
Emotional
Imagination
Domestic
Impulsive
Flexible
Positive
Magnetic
Protector
Romantic
Sociable
Inspiration, has
Inconstant
Negative
Mediumistic
Imitative
Dreamer
Frivolous
Worried

Materialistic

Weingarten
Receptivity
Emotional
Instinctive
Protector
Reflective
Fluctuates
Femininity
Sensitive
Adaptable
Changeable
Maternal
Sensitive, very
Passive

Mann
Femininity
Unconscious
Emotional
Instinctive
Reflective
Passive
Soul
Changeable
Fluctuates
Sensitive
Family, likes
Home, likes
Women, likes
Cooking, likes
Sea, likes the
Travel, fond of
Domesticated
Exteriorized
Formal
Beauty, likes

MERCURY KEYWORDS

Ptolemy
Intelligent
Well-advised
Docile
Informed
Subtle
Inventive
Experimenter
Reasoner
Ingenious
Imitator
Beneficent
Calculating
Speculative
Mathematics,
  likes
Mysterious
Success
Artful
Hasty
Oblivious
Impetus
Lightness
Changing
Conceited
Liar
Negligent
Unstable
Unfaithful
Unjust
Wicked
Bold
Rash

Carter
Communicative
Thoughtful
Speech
Writing

Letter writer
Business
Quick
Inquisitive
Expressive
Logical
Rapid
Details,
  attends to
Talkative
Brilliant
Imaginative, not
Exact
Facts, likes
Critical
Exaggerated
Sarcastic
Uncertain
Intellectual
Bad tempered

Hone
Communicative
Nervous
Spirituality
Reflective
Aptness
Coolness
Expressive
Details,
  attends to
Intelligent
Logical
Perceptive
Talkative
Artful
Critical mind
Diffuse
Inquisitive

Sly

Barbault
Winning manner
Adaptable
Movement, likes
Expressive
Intellectual
Brain worker
Supple
Skillful
Dexterous
Ingenious
Subtle
Changing
Varied
Unstable
Changeable
Bantering
Artful
Nervous
Translator
Secretary
Artisan
Commercial
Studies,
  brilliant
Traveller
Businessman
Financially
  motivated
Witty
Playing, likes
Lightness
Superficial
Journalist
Imitator
Parody
Pastiche
Conversationalist
Letter writer

Virtuoso
Libertine
Ironical
Cynical
Sarcastic
Critical sense
Drawer
Scientific

Hall
Educator
Cultured
Slender
Expressive
Penetrating
Nervous
Excited
Hasty
Brilliant
Superficial
Analytical mind
Intuitive
Skillful
Technician
Expressive
Reasoner
Thoughtful
Eloquent
Good memory
Affable
Witty
Literary
Dextrous
Subtle
Sensitive
Pleases
Impressionable
Gambler
Conceited
Clumsy
Communicative

Conscious
Magnetic
Spiritualism
Understanding
Secretary
Message
Journalist
Inventor
Orator
Industrialist
Letter writer
Message
Worried
Troublesome
Changes
Scatterbrained
Restless
Excited
Irregular
Mathematics
Traveller
Orator
Ambassador
Ingenious
Witticism
Commercial
Educator
Learned
Scientific
Inventor
Concrete
Constructive

Mayo
Communicative
Reasonable
Eloquent
Cunning
Inventive
Commercial
Perceptive
Sensations,
   open to

Exciting
Logical
Conscious
Coordination
Thinker
Interpreter
Message
Intellectual
Emotional, not
Changeable

Lee
Message
Quick
Imaginative
Studious
Sharp
Logical
Orator
Fretful
Worried
Conceited
Sarcastic

Grell
Reasoner
Message
Self-conscious
Perceptive
Observant
Communicative
Sensibility
Communicative
Free
Responsibilities,
   assumes
Self-conscious
Reflective
Expressive
Adaptable
Duality
Analytical
Emotional, not

Active
Educated
Scientific
Brilliance
Learned
Articulate
Precise
Observant
Resourceful
Dexterous
Refined
Detachment
Skeptical
Worried
Verbalism
Unstable
Critical
Impressionable
Inquisitive
Nervous
Imitator
Restless
Superior manners
Sympathetic, not

Weingarten
Communicative
Intellectual
Adaptability
Ideas, has

Various interests
Alert
Dexterous
Nervous
Gift of gab
Fidgety

Mann
Ambivalent
Intellectual
Communicative
Nervous
Dexterity
Ambiguous
Writing
Diplomat
Diffuse
Weak
Intellectual
Ambassador
Interpreter
Teaches
Psychologist
Listener
Sympathetic
Changeable
Instinctive
Duality
Critical

VENUS KEYWORDS

Ptolemy
Temperate
Overheated
Beneficent
Femininity
Noctambulist
Gracious
Glory
Honored
Peaceful
Children, likes
Friendships
Well-bred
Neat
Courteous
Religious
Influential
   friends, has
Affable
Good-natured
Loved
Eloquent
Jealous
Merry
Coddles himself
Artist
Agreeable
Benevolent
Grudge-bearing, not
Success
Voluptuous
Lazy
Love, in
Coward
Timid
Indifferent
Ribald
Quietly

Carter
Refined

Harmonious
Adaptable
Love
Understanding
Idealist
Universal
Collaboration
Unifying
Cooperative
Communal
Well balanced
Impartial
Placid
Refined
Artist
Sociable
Pleasure seeker
Loved
Working little
Happy
Harmonious
Lazy
Dependent
Careless
Lack of
   confidence
Dreaming
Lacks strength
Content
Affectionate
Apathetic
Indolence
Peaceful
Lack of
   moral courage

Hone
Harmonious
Unifying
Beauty, likes

Love
Affectionate
Businessman
Artist
Attractive
Love
Adaptable
Artistic
Companion
Gracious
Loving
Peaceful
Placid
Tactful
Artful
Love, worship
Languid
Lazy
Weak

Barbault
Attractive
Adhesion
Fusion
Youthful
Love, in
Tender
Beauty
Amusement, likes
Sensualist
Sensual
Aesthete
Caressing
Smiling
Gracious
Alive
Gay (Merry)
Affable
Soft
Sensitive
Elegant
Winning
Loving

Frivolous
Courtesan
Artist
Art, loves
Happy
Worldly
Merry
Peace, needs
Agreeable
Facility, has
Springy
Melodious poetry
Musical
Gallant

Hall
Warm
Femininity
Emotional
Sexuality
Graceful
Soft
Vivacious
Gracious
Patronizing
Negative
Depressed
Attachment
Perceptive
Analytical, not
Affectionate
Social action
Imaginative
Receptive
Beauty, likes
Cheerful
Suave
Friendships
Kind
Poetical
Artistic
Pleasure seeker
Harmonious

Sensual
Sentimental
Vain
Dissolute
Lazy
Superficial
Abandoned
Vulgar
Alluring
Conscious
Love
Unifying
Magnetic
Spiritualism
Musical
Painter
Poet
Actor
Domesticated
Love affairs
Attachments
Learned
Quarrels
Loved
Women, likes
Erotic
Outbursting
Artist
Sculptor
Prosperous
Loves art
Peaceful
Physical strength
Friendship
Continuity

Mayo
Unity of the work
Sympathetic
Loved
Beauty, likes
Productive work
Erotic

Harmonious
Warm
Passive
Steadfast
Serene
Rational, not
Inner life
Subjective
Femininity
Receptive
Soft
Unifying
Cooperative
Balanced, well
Smooth
Appreciated
Affective
Artist
Aesthete
Creative
Money, likes

Lee
Friendships,
  keeps
Altruistic
Beauty, likes
Harmonious
Affectionate
Sympathetic
Refined
Pleasure seeker
Sociable
Artistic
Soft
Smooth voice
Sensual
Lazy
Vain
Vulgar

Grell
Beauty, likes

Love
Femininity
Unifying
Loving
Artist
Harmonious
Cooperation
Refined
Love
Art
Sociable
Impressionable
Cooperative
Original
Musical
Romantic
Devoted
Refined
Harmonious
Companionable
Attractive
Responsibilities,
  assumes
Courteous
Considerate
Creative
Inspiration
Charming
Vain
Indulgent
Display
Attachment
Frivolous
Flirtatious
Sensitive, very
Indolent
Jealous

Weingarten
Attractive

Affectionate
Harmonious
Peaceful
Love
Artist
Beauty,
  likes
Gracious
Content
Ease
Graceful
Cooperative
Shares
Lazy
Vain
Flirtatious
Luxury,
  likes
Pacifist
Comfortable

Mann
Love
Harmonious
Artist
Feminine
Sexual
Attractive
Affectionate
Unifying
Beauty, likes
Erotic
Friendships
Companion
Sociable
Musical
Diplomatic
Pacifist
Romantic
Flatterer

MARS KEYWORDS

Ptolemy
Burning
Drive, full of
Masculine
Dry
Warrior
Violent
Generous
Choleric
Debauched
Robust
Courageous
Carefree
Persistent
Contemptuous
Tyrannical
Prompt
Command,
  sense of
Cruel
Unjust
Turbulent
Sumptuous
Shouts
Drinker
Pitiless
Fury
Enemy, has

Reckless
Excessive
Cruel
Brutal
Freedom, likes
Liberty, likes
Valiant
Idealistic
Fighter
Sudden
Assertive
Courage
Energy
Quarrelsome
Rough
Destructive
Egotism
Exuberant
Aggressive
Asserts himself
Noisy
Loud
Vain
Warm
Spirit
Enthusiastic
Timid, not
Sociable

Carter
Fiery
Energizing
Active
Enterprising
Push
Courageous
Muscular
Quick
Decision
Restless
Quarrelsome

Hone
Energetic
Active
Warrior
Initiator
Hot
Incisive
Courageous
Pioneer
Efforts
Initiative
Pugnacity

Courage
Energy
Asserts himself
Fighter
Materialistic
Combative
Constructive
Direct
Forces
  the success
Leader
Impulsive
Indignant
Passionate
Quick
Sexuality
Aggressive
Cruel
Destructive
Impatient
Pugnacious
Restless
Sensual
Thoughtless

Barbault
Strength
Conqueror
Tense
Impulsive
Desires
Violent
Maturity
Muscular
Choleric
Aggressive
Hates
Desires
Passionate
Energetic
Robust
Courageous
Virile

Combative
Prompt
Frank
Tyrannical
Sadistic
Rivalries
Enemies, has
Iron
Drive, full of
Hard
Cutting
Sharp pointed
Danger, likes
Passionate
Fighter
Dissipation
Litigant
Warrior
Critical sense
Polemist

Hall
Hot
Dry
Ambitious
Authority
Dignified
Military
Quick
Sharp
Ruddy
Fretful
Intolerant
Certain
Domineering
Energetic
Enthusiastic
Ardent
Pressing
Physical Strength
Acuteness
Penetrating
Active

Dynamic
Courageous
Forces
Enthusiastic
Fearless
Self-assurance
Brave
Impulsive
Gallant
Enterprising
Expert
Energetic
Magnanimous
Independent
Destructive
Passionate
Egotism
Coarse
Sarcastic
Ironical
Cruel
Quarrelsome
Warlike
Conscious
Dynamic
Energetic
Flame
Emotional
Perceptive
Desires
Military man
Metallic
Enemies, has
Adventurous
Burning
Glory
Impetuous
Violent
Outbursting
Excited
Sensibility
Excessive
Soldier

Mechanical
Strong
Aggressive
Rough
Warrior
Feverish
Dangerous
Terrible
Stormy
Contentious
Vitality
Combative
Secretiveness

Mayo

Activity
Enterprising
Asserts himself
Energetic
Physical Strength
Sensual
Initiator
Objective
Warrior
Muscular
Feverish
Cutting
Burning
Attacks
Resistant
Sexuality
Desires
Passionate
Iron
Warm
Active
Powerful
Emotional
Fighter
Pioneer
Cruel
Impatient
Destructive

Reckless
Impulsive
Aggressive

Lee
Greedy
Warrior
Force
Energy
Constructive
Courageous
Hot tempered
Aggressive
Grasping
Destructive
Impatient
Sensual
Coarse
Passionate
Cruel
Energetic

Grell
Desires
Energetic
Active
Dynamic
Builder
Progress, likes
Realist
Self-confidence
Self-discipline
Warrior
Hated
Heroic
Courageous
Experienced
Constructive
Self-willed
Sinner
Saintliness
Impulsive
Assertive

Courageous
Expressive
Independent
Forces
  the success
Practical
Enthusiastic
Dynamic
Generous
Aggressive
Heroic
Frank
Bold
Fearless
Devoted
Attachment
Determined
Domineering
Defiant
Violent
Combative
Egotist
Sarcastic
Obstinate
Passionate
Coarse
Cruel
Rash
Loud
Jealous
Destructive
Extreme

Weingarten
Active
Physical strength
Energetic
Sexuality
Aggressive
Militant
Impulsive
Direct
Initiative, has

Forces
  the success
Passionate
Courageous
Fighter
Arguer
Belligerent
Violent
Restless
Sensual
Hasty
Risky
Fearless
Overheated

Mann
Warrior
Changing
Conflict
Aggressive

Sexuality
Individualistic
Mannish
Strength, full of
Fighter
Metallic
Athletic
Mechanical
Technician
Male
Adventurous
Heroic
Egocentric
Assertive
Destructive
Materialistic
Worldly
Force
Desires

JUPITER KEYWORDS

Ptolemy
Temperate
Beneficent
Masculine
Glory
Abundant
Rest, likes
Peaceful
Superior manner
Liberal
Glory
Magnanimous
Religious
Jolly
Human
Splendid
Just
Greatness
Grave
Prolific

Prudent
Loving
Chief
Arrogant
Superstitious
Timid
Proud
Embarrasses
  others
Negligent
Reserved
Majestic
Frank

Carter
Kind
Sympathetic
Home, likes
Expansive
Philosopher

Scientific
Speculative
Generous
Hopeful
Loyal
Fortune,
  makes his
Excessive
Energetic
Optimistic
Faith, has
Reckless
Jovian
Pushes himself
  forward
Unreasonable
Gambler
Wasteful
Sporting
Hunter
Athletic
Animals, loves
Orderly
Healthy
Hopeful
Optimistic
Verbalism
Exuberant
Aggressive
Asserts himself
Noisy
Loud
Quarrelsome
Vain
Warm
Spirit
Idealistic
Enthusiastic
Timid, not
Sociable

Hone
Expansive
Cheerful

Jovial
Optimistic
Prosperous
Opportunist
Success
Sporting
Generous
Conversationalist
Jovial
Extremist
Improvident
Provocative
Wasteful

Barbault
Expansive
Asserts himself
Orderly
Coordination
Organizer
Authority
Jovial
Confiding
Optimistic
Spontaneous
Exteriorized
Breadth
Powerful
Vitality
Gourmand
Careless
Maturity
Protector
Beneficent
Spectacular
Happy
Comfortable
Successful
Success
Fortune, makes
Wondrous
Elevation
Honorary
  distinction

Power, has
Public man
Civil service
Religious
Justice, likes
Liberal
Peace, needs
Realistic
Warm
Humorous
Descriptive
Conventional
Bloated

Hall
Warm
Reflective
Prudent
Authority
Kind
Paternal
Temperate
Generous
Generalizing
Peaceful
Optimistic
Overcomes
  difficulty
Dramatic attitude
Beauty, likes
Common sense
Reasonable
Humane
Broadness
Expansive
Optimism
Idealistic
Religious
Sound judgment
Generous
Benevolent
Respectful
Honorable

Jovial
Sympathetic
Patient
Wise
Just
Popular
Extravagant
Dissipated
Conceited
Fanatic
Self-love
Critical, not
Irresolute
Lazy
Conscious
Idealist
Physician
Philanthropist
Success
Honors
Friendships,
  keeps
Dignified
Protector
Buoyant
Counselor
Wise
Rich
Mountebank
Dissipation
Aristocratic
Public man
Peaceful
Prosperous
Orderly
Constructive
Success
Content
Respectful
Abundant
Abstract
Creative
Sublime

Sublime
Mirth provoking

Mayo
Expansive
Powerful
Protector
Just
Virtue
Spreads out
Jovial
Conscious
Understanding
Maturity
Orderly
Morality
Religious
Fortune
Exaggeration
Extravagant
Conceited

Lee
Personality
Jovial
Happy
Expansive
Beneficent
Noble
Sincere
Kind
Religious
Honorable
Faithful
Extravagant
Conceited
Gambler
Hypocritical
Fanatical

Grell
Beneficent
Expansive

Optimistic
Promoter
Popular
Success
Generous
Confiding
 in others
Exaggerates
Extravagant
Conceited
Display, likes
Excessive
Active
Conservative
Religious
Philosopher
Orthodox
Rituals
Ceremonious
High conscience
Stimulating
Idealism
Tolerance
Understanding
Visionary
Dissipation
Benevolent
Jovial
Opportunist
Honorable
Tolerant
Humane
Formal
Idealistic
Philanthropist
Understanding
Devout
Revered
Ambitious
Faith, has
Radiant
Success
Popular

Vision
Charitable
Inspiring
Dignified
Excessive
Fanatical
Extremist
Indolent
Dissipation
Conceited
Pompous
Ostentatious
Display, likes
Successful

Weingarten
Expansive
Confidence
Generous
Magnanimous
Excessive
Jovial
Open
Liberal
Cheerful
Optimistic
Explorer
Opportunist
Extravagant
Wasteful
Show off
Haughty

Confident
Gambler
Hypocritical

Mann
King
Stormy
Beneficent
Justice, likes
Expansive
Warm
Optimistic
Generous
Religious
Philosopher
Fortune,
  makes his
Aristocratic
Official
Teaches
Individualistic
Enjoys life
Wise
Principles, has
Ideas, has
Reasoner
Meditative
Teacher
Guide
High conscience
Philosopher

SATURN KEYWORDS

Ptolemy
Masculine
Cold
Poor
Frightened
Careful
Greatness
Thinker
Deep
Sad
Solitary
Laborious
Imperious
Rich
Money, likes
Violent
Boring
Dirty
Lazy
Fearful
Fleeing
Backbiter
Complains
Imprudent
Superstitious
Peaceful
Melancholic
Uncivil

Carter
Justice, likes
Concrete
Practical
Materialistic
Patient
Hard working
Concentrated
Solid
Limited
Conservative
Narrow-minded
Mean
Selfish

Responsibilities,
   assumes
Sad
Hard working
Disappointment
Slow
Thorough
Prudent
Self-control
Worldly

Hone
Limited
Cold
Chilly
Patient
Difficulties,
   surmounts
Responsibilities,
   assumes
Old
Materialistic
Careful
Control, good
Just
Practical
Serious
Depressed
Dogmatic
Dull
Fearful
Grasping
Mean
Severe

Barbault
Concentrated
Abstract
Conservative
Contracted
Old, looks
Greedy
Jealous

Ambitious
Miser
Erudite
Inhibited
Renouncement
Self-controlled
Refusal
Timorous
Interiorized
Reserved
Prudent
Patient
Reflective
Calm
Deep
Stable
Serious
Faithful
Melancholy
Pessimistic
Selfish
Skeptical
Solitary
Sterility
Impotent
Masochist
Feels guilty
Eremite
Counselor
Philosopher
Learned
Wise
Mendicant
Native
   place, loves
Lab man
Responsibilities,
   takes
Bachelor
Fails
Sacrifice, spirit
Recluse
Late, always

Miserable
Abandonment
Hardworking
Traditional
Intransigent
Stiff
Tragic
Idyllic
Lyrical
Dramatic
Classical
Realistic
Cold
Romantic
Cursed

Hall
Cold
Dry
Resigned
Slender
Tenacious
Conventional
Secretive
Powerful
Authority
Tyrannical
Conservative
Faithful
Reserved
Inhibited
Self-controlled
Justice, likes
Orderly
Concrete
Technical
Details,
   attends to
Easily offended
Patient
Prudent
Scientific
Experimenter

Research worker
Mathematics
Faithful
Analytical mind
Systematic
Tactful
Responsible
Punctual
Chaste
Studious
Just
Pessimistic
Secretive
Avaricious
Suspicious
Jealous
Timid
Fatalistic
Egoism
Limited
Magnetic
Conservative
Habits
Secret
Friendships,
  keeps
Decadent
Fearful
Miser
Unwilling
  to speak
Narrow-minded
Poor
Prudent
Recluse
Clown
Landsman
Statesman
Administrator
Builder
Dignified
Self-esteem
Firm

Justice, likes

Mayo
Disciplined
Rigid
Limitation
Density
Structures
Acid
Hard
Slow
Coolness
Regular
Control, good
Dry
Discipline
Self-conscious
Clear mind
Logical
Concentrated
Concrete
Constructive
Builder
Contemplative
Monotonous
Laborious
Patient
Sense of duty
Serious
Reflective
Realistic
Practical
Resourceful
Egotism
Isolated
Fears difficulty
Suffers
Inhibited
Withdrawing
Selfish
Cruel
Depressive

Lee
Sad
Experienced
Limited
Wise
Reflective
Careful
Fearful
Economical
Laborious
Chaste
Morose
Suspicious
Nervous
Jealous
Timid
Fatalistic
Restrained

Grell
Justice, likes
Discipline
Perfection
Chase
Disappointed
Limited
Experienced
Patient
Humble
Wise
Compassionate
Destructive
Persistent
Self-discipline
Skeptical
Fearful
Materialistic
Confiding
 in others
Humble
Revered
Wise
Compassionate

Silent
Meditative
Concentrated
Restrained
Serious
Sincere
Defends himself
Details,
 attends to
Punctual
Stable
Moderate
Conventional
Observant
Humble
Responsibilities,
 assumes
Diplomatic
Revered
Systematic
Faithful
Wise
Fears
Sensitivity
Severe
Miser
Pessimistic
Exacting
Bitter
Narrow-minded
Rigid
Secretive
Selfish

Weingarten
Responsibilities,
 assumes
Discipline
Limited
Concentrated
Practical
Economical
Good control

Serious
Conservative
Ambitious
Frugal
Organizer
Slow
Patient
Thorough
Methodical
Logical
Meditative
Silent
Conformist
Loneliness, likes
Mistrust
Depressed
Inhibited
Fearful
Dull
Cold
Negative
Closed

Mann
Cold
Dry
Restrained

Depressive
Melancholy
Reserved
Limited
Serious
Economical
Authority
Acceptance
Concentrated
Discipline
Old
Authoritative
Dogmatic
Experienced
Objective
Independent
Unconscious
Withdrawing
Difficulty
 in life
Abnegation
Abstract
Negative
Materialistic
Equilibrated
Equalitarian

URANUS KEYWORDS

Ptolemy
No keywords

Carter
Energetic
Emotional
Intellectual
Original
Patience
Organizer
Common sense
Power, has
Responsibilities,
  assumes
Administrator
Official
Authority
Unconventional
Good natured
Outspoken
Rough
Crank
Fighter
Morbid
Sensitive
Explosive
Resentment
Bitter
Dangerous
Nervous
Peculiar
Sudden changes
Unexpected
Genius
Character, has
Perverse
Eccentric
Self-willed

Hone
Changeable
Freedom, likes
Changes
Unconventional

Crude
Intuitive
Inventive
Autocratic
Friendships
Magnetism
Original
Outspoken
Progress, likes
Reformer
Self-willed
Unconventional
Unusual,
  likes the
Occultist
Changeful
Attractive
Dangerous
Detached
Eccentric
Fascinating
Perverse
Rebel
Rough

Barbault
Tense
Impulsive
Awakens
Unity
Perky
Conspicuous,
  makes
Individualistic
Autonomy
Systematic
Asserts himself
Unity of work
Powerful
Authoritative
Intolerant
Independent
Peculiar

Original
Eccentric
Cynical
Extravagant
Maladjusted
Rebel
Agitated
Experimenter
Technician
Rationalist
Progress, likes
Reformer
Technician
Industrialist
Imperial
Fascist
Dictatorial
Aristocratic
Abstract
Spare style
Constructor
Dense
Absolute
Esotericism
Rational
Conscious

Hall
Warm
Slender
Pleasing
Ascetic
Impulsive
Eccentric
Fatalist
Scientific
Self-willed
Inner life
Active
Liberty, likes
Justice, likes
Leader
Pioneer

Independent
Original
Inventive
Unconventional
Altruistic
Sudden changes
Sensitive, very
Progress, likes
Humane
Intuitive
Prophet
Philosopher
Enthusiastic
Heroic
Perceptive
Spiritualism
Conscious
Awakener
Magnetism
Lecturer
Public man
Travel, fond of
Inventor
Aviator
Psychologist
Metaphysician
Sudden changes
Exiled
Impulsive
Tragic
Accidents
Enemies, has
Unexpected
Changes
Humanist
Speculates
Impostor
Aerial
Explosive
Anarchist
Invention
Occultist
Authority

Mayo
Inventive
Independent
Industrialist
Scientific
Discoverer
Magnetic
Changes faith
Unexpected
Excited
Convulsionary
Palpitating
Unstable
Spirituality
Clairvoyant
Homosexual
Perverse
Anarchist
Dramatic attitude
Genius
Intuitive
Creative
Original
Inspired
Freedom, likes
Imaginative
Altruism
Unorthodoxy
Rebellious
Reformer
Sexuality
Eccentric
Violent
Fanatical
Depraved
Peculiar

Lee
Rebel
Revolution
Freedom, likes
Warrior
Newness, likes

Sudden changes
Intuitive
Liberty, likes
Original
Abrupt
Bold
Romantic
Philosophical
Eccentric
Chaotic
Licentious
Sarcastic
Inordinate
Proud
Renouncement

Grell
Creative
Progress, likes
Unexpected
Awakener
Changeable
Unusual,
  likes the
Adventurous
Spectacular
Individualistic
Newness, likes
Scientific
Metaphysical tone
Occultist
Discontented
Tense
Inner life
Awake
Independent
Conformist, not
Original
Inventive
Unconventional
Altruistic
Idealistic
Reformer

Occultist
Friendships
Restless
Impulsive
Assertive
Sectarian, not
Progress, likes
Ingenious
Humane
Universal,
  sense of
Pioneer
Intuitive
Clairvoyant
Magnetism
Resourceful
Impersonal
Liberty, likes
Strong-minded
Abrupt
Rebellious
Visionary
Licentious
Dictator
Eccentric
Perverse
Bohemian
Vagabond
Fanatical
Tense

Weingarten
Free
Innovator
Sudden changes
Independent
Original
Unexpected
Excited

Inventive
Abrupt
Extremist
Individualistic
Independent
Unusual,likes the
Intuitive
Genius
Enthusiastic
Newness, likes
Rebellious
Wild
Defies
  conventions
Nervous
Eccentric

Mann
Patriarch
Sexuality
Eccentric
Inventive
Independence
Intuitive
Mobility
Peculiarity
Impulsive
Creative
Eccentric
Original, not
Rebel
Technician
Inspired
Independent
Innovator
Changing
Abstract
Universal
Metaphysical tone

NEPTUNE KEYWORDS

Ptolemy
No keywords

Carter
Delicate
Musical
Artistic
Idealist
Spirituality
Creative
Imagination
Inspired
Poet
Fanciful
Terrible
Pretentious
Deceptive
Staging, likes
Film
Spiritualism
Sensitive
Worried
Imposing
Subtle
Inspiration
Utopian

Hone
Impressionable
Hides
Veiled
Subversive
Kind
Spiritualism
Confusion
Mystic
Vague
Inspired
Unconscious
Artist
Dreamer
Emotional

Idealistic
Imaginative
Inspiration, has
Mediumistic
Sensitive
Spiritualism
Subtle
Careless
Deceptive
Sensitive, very
Sentimental
Subversive
Unstable
Wandering life
Wool gathering

Barbault
Engaged
Upright
Confusion
Receptive
Participate, need
Adhesion
Dissolute
Supersensitive
Emotional
Impressionable
Nuance
Diffuse
Uncertain
Imprecise
Charitable
Devoted
Sacrifice, spirit
Masochist
Escape, need to
Chimerical
Fleeing
Utopian
Idealist
Mystical
Sensitive, very

Intuitive
Mediumistic
Irrational
Surrealist
Collectivity,
  sense of
Group,
  member of a
Anarchist
Scandalous
Chaotic
Revolutionary
Popular
Trade unionist
Socialist
Lets himself go
Control, lack of
Effusiveness
Inspired
Lyrical
Confidence, makes
Fluid
Impressionist
Affectionate
Unconscious

Hall
Cruel
Mysterious
Hypnotism
Neurotic
Gloomy
Theatrical
Morbid
Conventional, not
Inconstant
Emotional
Fascinating
Penetrating
Musical
Romantic
Elfish
Clairvoyant
Mediumistic

Sarcastic
Erotic
Magnetic
Artist
Literary
Philosopher
Obsessional
Magician
Mystic
Wise
Eccentric
Genius
Prophet
Charitable
Intuitive

Mayo
Refined
Dissolution
Subtle
Immaterial
Evolves
Hypnotizes
Spirituality
Mysterious
Disturbed
Insane
Neurotic
Sensitive
Perceptive
Exciting
Inspired
Brilliant
Poet
Religious
Powerful
Hallucinated
Unconscious
Mediumistic
Impressionable
Idealist
Artist
Dreaming
Mystical

Humanist
Wool gathering
Practical, not
Confused
Chaotic
Vague
Obsessional
Illusionist
Desperate
Degraded
Drinker
Sexuality
Perverse
Neurotic
Homosexual

Lee
Mysterious
Romantic
Mystical
Introspective
Careless
Peaceful
Religious
Melancholy
Dreamy
Morbid
Inspired

Grell
Sensitivity
Deceptive
Sublime
Lower class
Sensitive
Secretive
Realistic, not
Dreamer
Dreams
Fantastic,
 likes the
Exotic
Bizarre
Tender

Romantic
Unrealistic
Mask
Wise
Reasoner, not a
Genius
Literary
Poet
Musical
Intuitive
Clairvoyant
Unifying
Vague
Obscure
Confusion
Misunderstood
Intrigue
Morbid
Introverted
Sensual
Obsessional
Sensitive, very
Idealistic
Impressionable
Emotional
Subtle
Abstract
Fanciful
Metaphysical
Spiritism,
 interested
Creative
Musical
Inspired
Sympathetic
Compassionate
Devoted
Imaginative
Revered
Poetic
Mystic
Spiritualism
Dreamy
Fearful

Negative
Immoral
Pretentious
Mediumistic
Chaotic

Weingarten
Idealist
Imaginative
Spirituality
Visionary
Impressionable
Inspired
Susceptible
Confused
Spiritualism
Idealistic
Romantic
Sensitive
Receptive
Open
Artistic
Compassionate
Mysterious

Resistant, not
Suggestible
Influences,
   susceptible to
Unrealistic
Disappointments
Pretentious
Dreamer

Mann
Mediumistic
Dreamer
Fantasy
Illusions, has
Sensitive
Alcoholic
Refined
Immaterial
Mystic
Unconsciousness
Obscure
Delicate
Illusionist
Solitary

PLUTO KEYWORDS

Ptolemy
No keywords

Carter
Hidden
Breaking off
Disturbs others
Isolated
Publicity, likes
Loneliness, likes

Hone
Renews his manner
Dark
Underground
Violent
Outbursting

Psychologist
Psychoanalyzed
Sexuality
Free
Deep
Revealing

Barbault
Transformation
Metamorphosis
Background,
   remains in the
Daemonic
Aggressive
Deep
Destroying

Anguished
Sacrifice, spirit
Mediumistic
Clairvoyant
Occultist
Symbolism
Psychoanalyzed
Sexuality

Hall
No keywords

Mayo
Transformation
Renewal
Creative
Deep
Unconscious
Colossal
Business
Enterprising
Obsessional
Neurotic
Outbursts
Violent
Destroys himself

Lee
Upsetting
Newness, likes
Introspective
Unsociable
Serious
Changeable

Grell
Transformation
Dictatorial
Active
Metaphysical tone
Occultism
Hypnotism
Change
Breaking off
Conformist, not

Intense
Group
Universal
Spiritualism
Clairvoyant
Destructive
Reckless
Fanatic
Invert
Sensual
Underground

Weingarten
Transformation
Power, has
Intense
Detached
Searcher
Destructive
Forces
Deep
Concentrated
Obsessional
Fanatic
Withdrawing
Distant
Cold
Machiavellian

Mann
Changing
Authoritarian
Revolutionary
Magician
Violent
Destructive
Fanatical
Magicians
Propagandist
Transformation
Unconscious
Reformer
Obsessional
Destruction
Self destructive

REFERENCES

Addey, J., Harmonics in Astrology, (Wisconsin: Cambridge Circle, 1976).

Addey, J., "Harmonic Phase and Personal Characteristics," The Astrological Journal, Summer 1979 & Winter 1979/80, (1979-1980).

Barbault, A., Défense et Illustration de l'Astrologie, (Paris: Grasset, 1955).

Barbault, A., Traité Pratique d'Astrologie, (Paris: Seuil, 1961).

Carter, C., The Principle of Astrology, (London: Theosophical Publishing House Ltd., 1971).

Couderc, P., L'Astrologie, (Paris: Presses Universitaires de France, 1974).

Gauquelin, M., "L'Astrologue pare de L'Ordinateur," Sciences et Vie, No. 611, (1968).

Gauquelin, M., Les Hommes et les Astres, (Paris: Denoël, 1960).

Gauquelin, M., L'Influence des Astres, (Paris: Editions du Dauphin, 1955).

Gauquelin, M., Cosmic Influences on Human Behavior, (New York: Stein & Day, 1973).

Gauquelin, M. & F., "Birth and Planetary Data Gathered Since 1949: Professional Notabilities, Series A, Vol. 1-6, (Paris: Laboratoire d'Etude des Relations entre Rhythmes Cosmiques et Psychophysiologiques, 1970-1971).

Gauquelin, M. & F., Méthodes pour étudier la répartition des Astres dans le Mouvement Diurne, (Paris: Laboratoire d'Etude des Relations entre Rythmes Cosmiques et Psychophysiologiques, 1957).

Gauquelin, M. & F., Psychological Monographs, Series C, Vol. 2-5, (Paris: Laboratoire d'Etude des Relations entre Rhythmes Cosmiques et Psychophysiologiques, 1973-1977).

Gauquelin, M. & F., Statistical Tests of Zodiacal Influences, (Paris: Laboratoire d'Etude des Relations entre Rhythmes Cosmiques et Psychophysiologiques, 1978).

Gauquelin, M. & F., The Venus Temperament, Series D, Vol. 4, (Paris: Laboratoire d'Etude des Relations entre Rhythmes Cosmiques et Psychophysiologiques, 1978).

Grell, P., Keywords, (Washington: American Federation of Astrologers, 1970).

Hall, M. P., Astrological Keywords, (Los Angeles: The Philosophical Research Society, 1966).

Hone, M., The Modern Textbook of Astrology, (London: Fowler & Co., 1978).

Ibn, Ezra A., Le Livre des Fondements Astrologiques, (Paris: Retz, 12th C.).

Lee, D., Dictionary of Astrology, (New York: Paperback Library, 1968).

Maternus, F., Mathesis, trans. Jean Rhys Bram, (Park Ridge, New Jersey: Noyes Classical Studies, 14th C.).

Mann, A. T., The Round Art, The Astrology of Time and Space, (Cheltenham, Great Britain: A Dragon World Book, 1978).

Mayo, J., *Teach Yourself Astrology*, (Great Britain: The English University Press, 1964).

Moore, M. & Douglas M., *Astrology, the Divine Science*, (York Harbour, ME: Arcane Publications, 1971).

Morin de Villefranche, J. B., *Astrologiae Gallicae*, trans. Jean Hieroz, (Paris: Omnium Littéraire, 17th C.).

Ptolemy, C., *Tetrabiblos*, trans. Nicolas Bourdin, rev. Rène Alleau, (Paris: Culture, Art, Loisir, 2nd C.).

Ptolemy, C., *Tetrabiblos*, III:9-10, trans. Robbins, (Cambridge: Loeb's Classical Library, Harvard University Press, 1956).

Rantzau, H., *Traité des Jugements des Thèmes Généthliaques*, (Nice, France: Cahiers Astrologiques, 17th C.).

Rodden, L., *Profiles of Women*, (U.S.A.: American Federation of Astrologers, Inc., 1979).

Weingarten, H., *The Study of Astrology*, (New York: A.S.I. Publications, 1977).

GAUQUELIN
PUBLICATIONS

**LABORATOIRE D'ETUDE DES RELATIONS ENTRE
RYTHMES COSMIQUES ET PSYCHOPHYSIOLOGIQUES
8, rue Amyot, 75005 Paris (France)**

Series A
Professional Notabilities

Volume 1: Sports Champions 1-2089		April 1970
Volume 2: Men of Science 1-3647		May 1970
Volume 3: Military Men 1-3439		July 1970
Volume 4: Painters and Musicians 1-2722		Nov. 1970
Volume 5: Actors and Politicians 1-2412		Dec. 1970
Volume 6: Writers and Journalists 1-2027		March 1971

Series B
Hereditary Experiment

Volume 1: Births 1-5011	Feb. 1970
Volume 2: Births 5012-9839	March 1970
Volume 3: Births 9847-13740	Sept. 1970
Volume 4: Births 13741-17499	Oct. 1970
Volume 5: Births 17500-21243	Jan. 1971
Volume 6: Births 21244-24949	Feb. 1971

Series C
Psychological Monographs

Volume 1: Profession-Heredity, statistical results of Series A & B	May 1972
Volume 2: The Mars Temperament & Sports Champions	May 1973
Volume 3: The Saturn Temperament & Men of Science	March 1974
Volume 4: The Jupiter Temperament & Actors	May 1974
Volume 5: The Moon Temperament & Writers	May 1977
Volume 6: A book of Synthesis	(to be published)

Series D
Scientific Documents

We calculate. . .You delineate!

CHART ANALYSIS

Natal Chart wheel with planet/sign glyphs. Choice of house system: Placidus (standard), Equal, Koch, Campanus, Meridian, Porphyry, or Regiomontanus. Choice of tropical (standard) or sidereal zodiac. Aspects, elements planetary nodes, declinations, midpoints, etc 2.00

Arabic Parts All traditional parts and more 1.00

Asteriods Ceres, Pallas, Juno and Vesta. Included in natal wheel + major planet aspects/midpoints . .50

Astrodynes Power, harmony and discord with summaries for easy comparison 2.00

Chiron, Transpluto or Lilith (only one) in wheel. . . . N/C

Concentric Wheels Any 3 charts available in wheel format may be combined into concentric wheels. 3.00
Deduct $1.00 for each chart ordered as a separate wheel.

Fixed Stars Robson's 110 fixed stars with aspects to natal chart 1.00

Graphic Midpoint Sort Proportional spacing highlights midpt. groupings. **Specify integer divisions of 360°** (1 = 360°, 4 = 90°, etc.) 1.00

Harmonic Chart John Addey-type. Wheel format, harmonic asc eq. houses. **Specify harmonic number** 2.00

Harmonic Positions 30 consecutive sets of positions **Specify starting harmonic number** 1.00

Heliocentric Chart Sun-centered positions 2.00

House Systems Comparison for 7 systems 50

Local Space planet compass directions (azimuth & altitude) plus Campanus Mundoscope 50

Locality Map USA or World map showing rise, upper & lower culmination and set lines for each planet . 6.00

Midpoint Structures Midpoint aspects + midpoints in 45° and 90° sequence 1.00

Rectification Assist 10 same-day charts **Specify starting time, time increment, i.e. 6 am, 20 minutes** 10.00

Relocation Chart for current location **Specify original birth data and new location** 2.00

Uranian Planets + half-sums. 50

Uranian Sensitive Points 3.00

HUMAN RELATIONSHIPS

Chart Comparison (Synastry) All aspects between the two sets of planets plus house positions of one in the other 1.50

Composite Chart Rob Hand-type. Created from midpoints between 2 charts. **Specify location** 2.00

Relationship Chart Chart erected for space-time mid-point between two births 2.00

COLOR CHARTS

4-Color Wheel any chart we offer in new, aesthetic format with color coded aspect lines 2.00

Local Space Map 4-color on 360° circle 2.00

Custom 6″ DIAL for any harmonic (laminated, you cut out) overlays on our color wheel charts 4.00

FUTURE TRENDS

Progressed Chart in wheel format. **Specify progressed day, month and year** 2.00

Secondary Progressions Day-by-day progressed aspects to natal and progressed planets, ingresses and parallels by month, day and year. **Specify starting year, MC by solar arc (standard) or RA of mean Sun.** . . . . 5 years 3.00
10 years 5.00
85 years 15.00

Minor or Tertiary Progressions Minor based on lunar-month-for-a-year, tertiary on day-for-a-lunar-month. **Specify year, MC by solar arc (standard) or RA of mean sun** . . . . 1 year 2.00

Progressed Lifetime Lunar Phases a la Dane Rudhyar. 5.00

Solar Arc Directions Day-by-day solar arc directed aspects to the natal planets, house and sign ingresses by month, day and year. **Specify starting year.** Asc and Vertex arc directions available at same prices. 1st 5 years 1.00
Each add'l 5 years .50

Primary Arc Directions includes speculum 5 years 1.50 **Specify starting year** . . . . . . Each add'l 5 years .50

Transits by all planets except Moon. Date and time of transiting aspects/ingresses to natal chart. **Specify starting month.** Moon-only transits available at same prices. . . . . 6 mos. 7.00
12 mos. 12.00
summary only, 6 mos. 3.50
summary only, 12 mos. 6.00

Outer Planet Transits Jupiter thru Pluto 12 mos. . . 3.00

Returns in wheel format. All returns can be precession corrected. **Specify place, Sun-return year, Moon-return month, planet-return month.**
Solar, Lunar or Planet 2.00
13 Lunar 15.00

Custom Graphic Ephemeris in 4 colors. **Specify harmonic, zodiac, starting date.**
1 or 5 YR TRANSITS with or without natal 5.00
1 or 5 YR TRANSITS, NATAL & PROGRESSED . . 7.00
85-YR PROGRESSIONS with natal positions . . 10.00
NATAL LINES ONLY (plus transparency) 4.00
additional natal (same graph) 1.00
additional person's progressions (same graph) . 2.00

POTPOURRI

Custom House Cusps Table For each minute of sidereal time. **Specify latitude ° ′ ″** 10.00

Custom American Ephemeris Page Any month, 2500BC-2500AD. Specify zodiac (Sidereal includes RA & dec.)
One mo. geocentric or two mos. heliocentric . . . 5.00
One year ephemeris (**specify beginning month, year**) 50.00
One year heliocentric ephemeris 25.00

Fertility Chart The Jonas method with Sun/Moon squares/oppositions to the planets, for 1 year. **Specify starting month** 3.00

Lamination of 1 or 2 pages 1.00
Transparency (B/W) of any chart or map 1.00
Handling charge per order 2.00

SAME DAY SERVICE

ASTRO COMPUTING SERVICES
P.O. BOX 16430
SAN DIEGO, CA 92116-0430
NEIL F. MICHELSEN